Break on Through
TO THE OTHER SIDE

A true story—as told by the one who survived it.

Marty Berry

Copyright © 2015 Marty Berry

All rights reserved.

ISBN: 1494933055

ISBN 13: 9781494933050

Library of Congress Control Number: 2014900432

CreateSpace Independent Publishing Platform

North Charleston, South Carolina

Dedication

Break On Through To The Other Side is dedicated to all the hurting broken people wherever they may be found in their journey of life.

"Hope can be a pleasant companion, who holds your hand while your other hand reaches into the future, free of the gravity of the moment, to bring back a dream for the waiting, waking world to see." Marty Berry

Spencer,

Everyone has a story and your story will be worth telling as you continue to grow in grace and stature. Your potential is great and will be full of adventure. Your genuine care & concern for people will influence many lives. All the best!

Love Ya, Uncle Bear

Table of Contents

Story 1:	*Light My Fire*	*1*
Story 2:	*One Fine Spring Day*	*6*
Story 3:	*Down Side Up*	*10*
Story 4:	*Jesus Freaks*	*15*
Story 5:	*Unintended Consequences*	*21*
Story 6:	*Everything Had Changed*	*26*
Story 7:	*Light Up My Life*	*30*
Story 8:	*Forty Acres of Marijuana*	*35*
Story 9:	*Got Milk?*	*40*
Story 10:	*On the Road Again*	*45*
Story 11:	*Drugs & Guns*	*53*
Story 12:	*Behind Bars*	*58*
Story 13:	*Out on Bail*	*63*
Story 14:	*Maui Wowi*	*69*
Story 15:	*Get Out of Dodgendorf*	*73*
Story 16:	*Escape to Ios*	*77*
Story 17:	*The Island Is Ours*	*80*
Story 18:	*Bombs Away*	*83*
Story 19:	*Kibbutz Gonen*	*87*
Story 20:	*Jerusalem, Jerusalem*	*91*
Story 21:	*To Die or Not to Die?*	*99*
Story 22:	*Does the "I Am" Care?*	*103*
Story 23:	*Springtime*	*109*
Story 24:	*Diversity & Harmony in Switzerland*	*115*
Story 25:	*One for All & All for One*	*121*
Story 26:	*Honey & the Bear*	*127*
Story 27:	*Summer Olympics*	*135*

Story 28:	*Hello America, I'm Back*	*141*
Story 29:	*Anamosa State Penitentiary*	*148*
Story 30:	*The Yard*	*152*
Story 31:	*Marty the Monk*	*156*
Story 32:	*War in the Dungeon*	*160*
Story 33:	*Welcome to the Neighborhood*	*164*
Story 34:	*Big Bad John*	*169*
Story 35:	*Receiving & Discharge*	*173*
Story 36:	*Welcome to the Cuckoo's Nest*	*177*
Story 37:	*Apomorphine, Anyone?*	*181*
Story 38:	*Miracles Do Happen*	*185*
Story 39:	*Open the Doors*	*190*
Story 40:	*The New Day Begins*	*196*
Epilogue		*203*

References:

Uncle Bear

You will notice at the beginning of each story there is a quote signed, Uncle Bear. I am the bear. Matt, Mindy's younger brother, was playing high school basketball. We went to see him play. Mindy and I arrived a few minutes late to the game. When we walked in to the gymnasium the stands were full of cheering fans.

I was wearing a rustic leather coat. My hair was abundant and my bread was bountiful. The movie The Life and Times of Grizzly Adams had just come out in theaters. Not a few teenagers began to call out to me, "Grizzly Adams! Grizzly Adams! Grizzly, Grizzly." From that day forward Matt has called me Bear and has never referred to me as Marty

My nieces and nephews have called me Uncle Bear for over thirty years, and counting. To my surprise and delight, others have included me into their extended families and they too call me their Uncle Bear.

Nàmes and Timeline

Some of the names of the characters were changed in order to protect the guilty and a few innocent people. You will notice a prevalence of nicknames given to many of my childhood friends. I think this peculiarity might have risen from our amusement with a film series known as *Our Gang*.

The timeline has been carefully preserved in order to replicate accurately the events from story to story. However, a few adjustments to the timeline were made to accommodate each story flowing as seamlessly as possible throughout the manuscript. The metaphoric personality of Misty Misery represents a number of female acquaintances condensed into one character. Hers was the only character for which this was done in the entire manuscript.

Photographs

All photographs pertaining to the Forty Stories are black and white film taken over forty years ago. I do so wish the photos could have been of a better quality. Frankly, it was hard enough finding photos that were forty years old.

The Invitation

The sixties era began for many of us on a day that appeared to be as mundane and routine as any other date on the calendar. However, it turned out to be a day that would leave a wound in the hearts and minds of millions. Three passionate, highly visible, iconic notables died on that day. On November 22, 1963, the spirit and energy of life was altered in America and around the world.

I was fourteen years old. The school lunch period had just begun. A friend and I snuck off campus to meet his older brother. He was waiting for us down the street from the school in his '55 Chevy. We pretty much ditched lunch, a class, or school, for that matter, whenever we felt like it. The vice principal of Sycamore Junior High School referred to me as his "hoodlum intellectual."

We climbed into my friend's older brother's groovy Bel Air, and cruised around the neighborhood. The radio blared surfer rock music and we each lit up a Lucky Strike cigarette

Right in the middle of Van Morrison's song "Gloria," the music stopped. A stern, yet subdued voice came on the radio and said, "This is Walter Cronkite reporting." His voice cracked; he was obviously distraught about something. He continued, "Today at one o'clock central standard time, John F. Kennedy, the president of the United States, has been assassinated. The president of the United States is dead. It is official, the president is dead."

After pulling the car over to the curb and stopping, we sat in motionless silence. We could not believe our ears, but the radio announcer was Walter Cronkite, the most trusted newscaster in America. We headed back to the campus.

Upon entering the lunch area, I began to yell, "*The president is dead! John F. Kennedy has been assassinated! Our president is dead!*"

A couple of my schoolmates laughed, thinking I was just screwing around. One of my female interests looked at me with an angry glare, and said, "Marty, that isn't funny!"

Another girl said, "Marty Berry, you can be such a jerk!"

Nobody wanted to believe me. Nobody did believe me. I continued my declaration, "*The president is dead! John Kennedy has been assassinated!*"

It took a few minutes before the atmosphere changed. A strange tension filled the air. Everyone appeared to have slowed down; they looked like mimes in an eerie dream.

Nevertheless, I yelled again, "*I'm telling the truth! The president is dead! I'm telling the truth!*"

Finally, after several minutes had passed, the school intercom system blared out the official announcement.

There was an awful silence for several seconds. Then I could hear cautious whispering and the vague whimpering sound of weeping. A girl standing near me timidly repeated one word over and over again, "Why? Why? Why?"

Most historians have placed the sixties era as being 1964 through 1974. However, I believe on that day, November 22, 1963, the iconic era of the sixties counterculture revolution began in our hearts and souls. The sleeping giant of the baby boom generation had been crudely and distressfully awakened to a new era on the day our dearly beloved President John F. Kennedy was assassinated.

On the same day JFK died, two other iconic individuals passed into eternity. Quite naturally, the deaths of C. S. Lewis and Aldous Huxley were not publicized or covered at any length, due to the passing of John F. Kennedy. Nevertheless, the writings of Huxley and Lewis have had a tremendous influence on the lives of millions. Huxley is best known for his 1932 novel, *Brave New World*, and his psychedelic book, *The Doors of Perception*. C. S. Lewis, the Irish-born novelist, poet, and medievalist, is best known for his fictional work, especially *The Chronicles of Narnia*, and for his nonfictional work, *Mere Christianity*.

After the day these three men died, it didn't take much time for the seeds of fear, discontent, and insecurity to germinate, break through and grow into a full-blown cataclysmic shift in the youth culture of America, and around the world.

The sixties were a time of moving beyond the norm, and experimenting with anything and just about everything, including drugs, sex, spirituality, religion, education, music, fashion, length of hair, and so on. It was a time of breaking through for millions of us. Unfortunately, not all breakthroughs were positive.

Huxley, in his later years, wrote *The Doors of Perception.* Jim Morrison named his band The Doors after the title of Huxley's book. No one would have been more surprised than Huxley to find his photograph among those on the cover of the Beatles' album *Sgt. Pepper's Lonely Hearts Club Band* four years after he passed from this world to the next.

I participated in the mystique of the "turn on, tune in, and drop out" movement popularized by Timothy Leary's slogan. Dr. Leary having served as a professor at Harvard University and Berkeley University was once described by President Richard Nixon as the most dangerous man in America.

Leary enjoyed hanging out with the legendary Brotherhood of Eternal Love. The founder of the Brotherhood, John Griggs, lived and grew up just down the street from me in East Anaheim.

The Brotherhood of Eternal Love produced and sold more LSD than anyone else in the world. Some of the law officers in Orange County, California, called them the Hippie Mafia, a label that was humorous and unfounded, in that their only weapons were peace, love, and Orange Sunshine LSD.

"Break on Through to the Other Side" was one of the hit songs by the infamous psychedelic rock band The Doors from their debut album in 1967. I chose this song as the metaphoric title of my book because it represents an immense inventory of diverse mystical and spiritual possibilities.

I also selected it because it is a musical signature of the sixties. A popular song can so often be a hidden calendar, safely tucked away in our musical memories.

As I mentioned, not all breakthroughs of the sixties were positive. Jim Morrison, Jimmy Hendrix, and Janice Joplin never saw their thirtieth birthdays. They all passed into eternity from drug and alcohol-related tragedies.

The sixties were my time to *Break on Through to the Other Side,* from the ritual of everyday life to the realm of mystery and spiritual awakening. My personal journey of transformation is the progressive theme of my stories. I am not a writer. I am a storyteller. I hope you enjoy my stories, as we journey back to the wild, wonderful, and tragic days of the sixties.

Story 1:
Light My Fire

The breath that removes the light of a candle arouses the flame of a campfire.
—Uncle Bear

I threw another log on the campfire. The fire roared back, with embers bursting into sparks they did fly. Little more than an hour earlier, during a dismal, overcast sunset, we had gathered some nearby river rocks and placed them in a circle. Our newly formed fire pit was only a few feet from the banks of the rapid Slocan River.

After stoking the fire, I sat with my feet dangling over the riverbank's edge. While gazing into the swift-moving, ice-cold water, I wondered, "*How in the hell did I end up here in the Kootenay Mountains of British Colombia, planting forty acres of marijuana?*"

No answer immediately came to mind. So I relaxed a little and took a deep breath of the fresh mountain air. I settled into the sound of the crackling fire and the mesmerizing flow of the river as it passed before me. I drifted off into the realm of remembrance, where time rides on the wings of the imagination.

Random movie clips of my younger years spun through my mind's eye. With no real effort on my part, a collection of life reels from the '60s were projected in random sequence for my viewing pleasure. All sorts of weird stuff and journeys of days gone by were rolled out from my personal video vault. I was caught off guard by an awkward sense of not belonging to the present moment.

Some of my old memories were shadowed by anxiety over what the future might hold. Even though the clips were many years old, I could still feel the emotions of worry, fear, and uncertainty. I'm not sure how people viewed me, but under the surface, I was apprehensive and defensive. I don't know if I ever really trusted anyone.

Two voices were perched on my shoulders. The voice on my left shoulder was shame, the one on my right, failure. They kept reminding each other why they deserved to occupy their individual territory near my ears. I had developed a strange habit of listening to them. I felt that I was at the end of my beginning, or at the beginning of a new ending. In either case, I was confused about where my life was headed.

Money, or getting money, had become an obsession with me. The obsession started innocently enough, with the fascination of actually being paid for things I could do. I was twelve years old when I landed my first paying job, washing delivery trucks on Saturdays at a food-packing plant right off the I-5 freeway in East Anaheim. My boss was not exactly a sterling personality. He did pay me fifty cents an hour in cash under the table, as they say, for my efforts. I thought that was pretty cool, considering minimum wage was $1.25 an hour in 1960. Somehow the seeds of greed were unconsciously planted in my heart at that time.

One particularly warm Saturday afternoon, I had finished washing the delivery trucks early. I was actually too young to be working legally. However, in Animal-heim, just about everything was doable in the early '60s, and I was a hard worker. On that Saturday afternoon, I asked my boss if there was anything else I could do for the next couple of hours.

He led me inside the food-packing plant, opened the janitor's closet, pointed inside, and said, "Just sweep up and mop the floors, and stay out of trouble!" I had no way of knowing this would be my last day working at the food-packing plant.

After about an hour of sweeping and mopping my way around the inside of the plant, I came across a pile of guts, gore, and the bloody

Story 1: Light My Fire

remains of various livestock on the floor. The heap of bloody guts and gore looked to be at least three feet high, with a well-footed shovel stuck in the middle of the mess.

I looked around for a big trash can, and found a fifty-five gallon plastic can that had four wheels for rolling it in any direction you pleased. I rolled it to the pile of remains, and had started to shovel the gore into the trash can when, to my startled surprise, a black man all dressed in white, including a big white chef's hat, came walking toward me with fearful determination.

He yelled at me, "Hey you, shrimp cocktail! What are you doin' with my hot dogs?"

I spoke without thinking, "*What hot dogs?*"

"The dogs that you are shoveling into that trash can; that's what dogs I'm talkin' about."

I was scared stiff, "*I'm sorry sir. I thought it was just guts and stuff.*"

When my boss got wind of the encounter I'd had with the hot dog chef, he told me that I could never return to the food-packing plant. I promised him I wouldn't tell a living soul about the hot dogs, but he said it was too late, I could not return.

I had various other jobs during the following years, from delivering newspapers to cleaning construction sites. At sixteen, I worked an eight-hour shift six nights a week, at the Hancock gas station on the corner of State College Boulevard and Lincoln Street in East Anaheim.

I liked having money in my pocket, and especially in my own bank savings account. Most of what earnings I did spend went into my first car, a 1959 cream yellow El Camino truck. It had an inlaid white stripe down the side, with impressive whitewall tires and a classy, white snap-down tarp covering the truck bed.

You needed a vehicle if you wanted to do any serious dating. I was somewhat of a scoundrel during my teenage years. At seventeen, I had three girlfriends all at the same time; one lived in Fullerton, another in Santa Ana, and the third lived in Anaheim. I dated more than a few girls during my instructive formative years.

Break on Through to the Other Side

Although I dated a good number of delightful, attractive girls, in my heart of hearts I knew I had not yet had the pleasure of meeting the love of my life. I had no idea at the time how long it would take, or where in the world I would find her. But I knew she was out there somewhere, and that much of my life would depend on finding her.

I tried to imagine what she might look like, as my thoughts continued to drift with the flow of the Slocan River. I listened to the soothing sounds of the rapidly passing waters as they sought for the larger waterways yet to be discovered. Within minutes, my wandering thoughts returned to the landscape of teenage years gone by.

After attending, well actually, after being thrown out of three different schools my senior year, I did finally graduate from Anaheim High School. Mainly because none of the other high schools in Anaheim wanted me back the next year. No college scholarship was waiting for me. I had just turned eighteen. I was now eligible for the draft, and most likely would be sent off to war in Vietnam.

Through the grapevine, I had heard about a guy named David O'Brien. He and three of his buddies had burned their draft cards on the steps of the South Boston District Courthouse in 1966. They were forthwith seized by police, ushered into the courthouse, and arrested by FBI agents. The case made its way through the lower courts, with the Supreme Court eventually hearing and ruling on it. David Paul O'Brien was convicted for *only* burning his draft card, and sentenced to the maximum of six years in federal prison as a youth offender.

I had friends older than me who had already gone to war, and returned in body bags. The apparently more fortunate friends who returned alive from Vietnam were, for the most part, really screwed up in their heads.

For the life of me, I could not see why I should travel halfway around the world to Vietnam and kill a bunch of short people I had never met. They didn't pose a national threat to our country, nor was my family in any present danger.

Story 1: Light My Fire

So I made up my mind; I was going to be a draft dodger. I would live with the shame of knowing that it would hurt my dad, a proud World War II veteran. It meant I would probably need to leave the United States for possibly many years to come, maybe forever.

That's when my view of life in America changed, and it would never be the same. One thing was certain—my attitude and perspective had radically shifted. It was as if I had put on a pair of glasses that altered the way I saw everything.

I had no idea at the time that my future life would include fleeing the United States as a fugitive, with considerable danger, facing life-threatening situations, living precariously in Canada, Europe, and the Middle East, wanted by the FBI, and facing a thirty-year sentence for conspiracy to overthrow the United States government.

Story 2:
One Fine Spring Day

Remembering my worldview or opinion regarding anything is hard enough without needing to remember my reason for having it in the first place.
—Uncle Bear

I was just beginning to discover a hard life lesson at that point. It is not *what* you think you see that eventually forms your world-view; rather, it is *how* you see what you observe that will ultimately form your perception of reality.

In many ways, it was easy for me to make the transition from being a Southern California surfer dude to that of a far-out hippie. As surfers, we loved nature, long hair, beer or wine, girls, and crazy stupid fun. So what was there to change to become a hippie?

I had turned eighteen years of age on May 17. On a classic Southern California spring day in 1967, I rode my brother Jonnie's 250 Honda Scrambler motorcycle to the nearby hills and canyons of Silverado, Modjeska, Trabuco, and my favorite, Black Star Canyon. Black Star was the most remote and hardest to navigate.

Hidden within the sandstone walls of Black Star Canyon was a wonderful secret that few had discovered. The overgrowth of bushes and trees made it almost impossible to find the clandestine surprise by walking upstream from the beginning of the canyon. However, there was a dirt path along the canyon cliff that a motorcycle could maneuver.

Story 2: One Fine Spring Day

After climbing in first and second gear for nearly a mile parallel to the canyon, a single stone marker signaled the way to high ground and the awaiting unexpected delight. After a quick five-minute scamper through the brush and trees, I found myself looking over the edge of a majestic, tranquil waterfall.

It was a sight to behold. The waterfall delicately drifted downward for more than a hundred feet to the polished, round stones that endlessly sang the song of the mountain springs.

I crossed the pristine creek by leaping from one stepping-stone to another. On the far side of the creek was a slippery slope of a path that had to be carefully navigated on the descent to the floor of the canyon. I was alone in the canyon at the waterfall on this particular spring day. I smoked a joint and drank a little red wine, accompanied by some bread and cheese.

I sat in silence for several minutes, trying to just be in the moment. A euphoric calm came over me as I gazed into the tumbling cascade of the gently falling water, and listened to the constant calming chorus of the waterfall splashing on the rocks. The beauty of the surroundings, and the fresh cool mist in the air, renewed my outer and inner self.

Seemingly from nowhere, and from everywhere, a question came softly into my thoughts: *What is truth?* I spontaneously blurted out the words, "*What is truth?*" No answer came to mind. I pondered the question for several minutes, and then kind of lost track of time. I drifted off in my thoughts to a place I call *no-man's land-mind*, which is at the end of the open territory of thought, and where the random chaos of mindless repetition begins.

I was brought back to the present moment by the same question: *What is truth?* The question focused my attention on the here and now. Remaining centered, I continued to ask myself the question, without effort, throughout the day. The question swirled, undulating deeper into my soul: *What is truth? What is truth? What is truth?*

The inquiry gently continued for several days. In my younger years, I had wondered from time to time what the truth about life actually was—where we came from, why we were alive, and where we went when we died. I asked several other people that week if they knew what the truth was. To my disappointment, no one seemed to know the answer, or even why I was asking the question.

Eighteen year old Marty at Black Star Canyon waterfall

The weekend could not have come fast enough. Saturday had finally arrived, a few of my friends and I headed out to Black Star Canyon. Most of us had motorcycles of one sort or another, and those who didn't had to ride, with a little embarrassment, on the back of someone else's bike.

All of us arrived and safely made our way down the wet, slippery slope to the bottom of the canyon. We put a bag of fruit in the

Story 2: One Fine Spring Day

cold water at the base of the waterfall. We drank a little red wine, and smoked a pipe of marijuana with a little hashish mixed in. I began pondering, once again, the same thought that had been softly haunting me for several days: *What is truth?*

Story 3:
Down Side Up

*You are finally free when you have forgotten
where you put your fears.*
—Uncle Bear

The sunshine was now directly overhead in the canyon, and the mist from the waterfall on my face felt magical. It wasn't unusual for one or more of my friends to bring along a book from the Tao or Buddhism, the Bible, or whatever anyone thought might be spiritually trippy. Sad Alan—he had droopy eyes—had brought what looked to be a miniature book of some sort.

"*Dude, what's in that little black book?*" I asked.

"It's the New Testament and Psalms from the Bible," he replied.

"*Far-out! I dig Jesus. Let's check out what he had to say in that little black book.*"

We had no problem with Jesus. He was cool with his long hair and sandals, and he wore a robe. I really didn't know much about Jesus but I did think he was groovy. Basically, I knew that he talked about love and peace, and then they killed him.

I didn't realize that Jesus Christ was an actual person until I was somewhere around six or seven years old. I had thought Jesus Christ was a swear word. I can't remember meeting anyone who said he or she was simply a Christian. Most people would say something like, "I'm a Methodist," "I'm a Catholic," "I'm a Mormon," or some other religious affiliation.

Story 3: Down Side Up

Jimmy's family was of the Christian Science persuasion of faith. One time, Jimmy's sister Sandy lay in bed for a week with a broken leg. Her parents kept telling her it was all in her head, and she just needed to reject the idea that her leg was broken. After the week passed and her leg was still broken, they took her to the doctor to set her leg. I, and the other kids, thought Jimmy's parents were as crazy as hell. I think Sandy agreed with us.

I turned my attention back to Sad Alan. "*Alan, read to us from the little book.*"

"Where do you want me to read from?"

I had no idea where to tell him to read from. I had never read the New Testament, or the Bible, for that matter. "*Just open it anywhere and read from it.*"

He opened the little book and started to read these words: "Let not your heart be troubled; you believe in God, believe also in me. In my father's house are many mansions. If it were not so, I would have told you. I go to prepare a place for you."

I interrupted him, "*Who is doing the talking?*"

"These are the words of Jesus," replied Alan.

"*How do you know they are the words of Jesus?*"

Sad Alan hesitated and then replied, "Because they are printed in red ink."

I was a little confused, so I asked, "*Why are they printed in red ink?*"

Sad Alan had no idea. He just shrugged his shoulders and said, "I guess so that we will know when Jesus is doing the talking."

Sarcastically, I replied, "*Are Christians that stupid that they have to have his words printed in red to know when he is speaking?*"

Jimmy chirped into the conversation, "No, you damn idiot. That is just the way it is done."

I personally thought the words of Jesus were a little odd. "*Why is he going somewhere to prepare a place for them?*" I asked. No one seemed to know. I was a little irritated at the confusion. Nevertheless, I was kind of intrigued by his not-so-clear words.

Sad Alan continued to read, "I will come again and receive you to myself that where I am there you may be also. Thomas, one of the Apostles, said to him, Lord, we do not know where you are going and how can we then know the way?"

I laughed out loud and remarked, "*So! I'm not the only one who doesn't know what the hell he is talking about.*"

Alan was getting really irritated at me, "Marty, do you want me to read this or not?"

"*I'm sorry, man. Yeah, please read on.*"

Sad Alan composed himself, and continued reading, "Jesus said to him, I am the way, the truth, and the life."

I could not believe my ears. I sat up straight, stretched out my hand, and demanded, "*Alan, hand me the book so I can read it for myself.*"

Everyone roared with laughter at me, but Sad Alan was not amused. He scornfully looked me in the eye and asked, "Marty, what in the hell is wrong with you today?"

"*Could you please just hand me the book so that I can read it with my own two eyes?*"

Sad Alan extended his arm in my direction, with the book still open to the place where he was reading, and said, "John fourteen verse six is where I tried to read from."

I read it silently, and then I read it out loud. Sad Alan had read it correctly. Jesus did say that he was the truth. I was dumbfounded and amazed. I sat silently for several seconds while I tried to grasp the meaning of the words, "I am the truth."

As I pondered, it occurred to me that Jesus might have been a crazy nut-case prophet or maybe just some whacked-out dude. On the other hand, what if he really was the way, the truth, and the life? I felt really uncomfortable, and a little irritated with the dilemma of the various contradictions of the words of Jesus. I thought the truth would be some kind of reasoning about philosophy or maybe a moral absolute—not some kind of mystical metaphor.

Story 3: Down Side Up

It had never entered my mind that a person could be the truth. I asked the others, "*Has anyone else ever said they were the way, the truth, and the life?*" No one in our little circle could think of anyone who had ever claimed such stuff. I was skeptical, but at the same time, I was curious for the first time in my life about this guy called Jesus. I wondered, *Is it possible that the truth could be a person, and not a concept, belief, or religion?*

That night, as I lay in bed with my bedroom door closed, I pondered how completely irrational it would be for Jesus, a person, to be the truth. However, my curiosity ran to the depths of my soul, and from deep within me, the question echoed back to me ever so faintly, *What is truth?*

I felt the sensation of a breath or a gentle breeze pass over my face. I looked to see if my window was open; it was not. I knew somehow that a spirit had just passed by me. I tried to relax, and whispered these words, "*Is Jesus Christ really the truth?*" I pondered those words over and over again, until a very strange thing took place. I had an experience I can only describe as a voice speaking to me. The voice didn't speak audibly, but in my thoughts. It was otherworldly, not like anything I had experienced before. It was Spirit, and I knew the voice was not my own thoughts.

The voice spoke these words, "Jesus is who he said he was." I sensed a presence in the room with me. My mental defense system was quick to react to the voice with these thoughts: *Marty, you have lost your mind. You have completely flipped out. You have now entered psycho-land at Disneyland. Your mother told you that drugs would destroy your brain.*

I tried to calm myself, and took a few slow, deep breaths of air. The voice spoke again in my mind, with soft reassuring words, "You are not crazy. The Christ is who he said he was."

I reacted with a question, *How in the world do I get to know the truth?*

"Embrace the truth," encouraged the voice.

I immediately experienced a strange embarrassment, and felt somewhat silly, but nevertheless, for no apparent reason, I started to gently weep. I felt a warm, loving presence covering me like a soft, silk, weightless down comforter. I knew intuitively in my heart that the voice and the presence was the Spirit of the Eternal One. "Ask for him" coaxed the voice.

Through my tears I whispered these words, "*Jesus, if you are the truth, please make yourself known to me.*" No sooner did the words leave my lips, than I experienced a feeling of love, and an emotion of security beyond my ability to describe. It was like I fell into the softness of belonging and the total acceptance of the Eternal Spirit.

The tears continued to gently flow for several minutes. Then a stranger thing happened—I started to laugh. I laughed and laughed, until exhausted. I fell asleep with a smile on my face.

Story 4:
Jesus Freaks

*Letting go of the death grip of fear, living in al-oneness,
usually follows touching the light lightly
in a calming sense of oneness.*
—Uncle Bear

During the months to come, I met hundreds of hippies who in wanting to know the truth, stumbled upon Jesus. However, things were getting a little weird and out of control. There were many new would-be followers of Jesus, but very few spiritually seasoned people to guide us.

One morning, Termite—he had buckteeth, and liked to chew on just about anything—came to my front door and enthusiastically pounded on it. I opened the door and asked, "*What's up, Termite?*"

"Marty, I just finished reading the book of palms and it was very cool, but I totally don't get the book called job. It doesn't mention anything about his job, and why do they keep calling him job? What does his work have to do with anything, anyway?"

After I stopped laughing, I explained that he had mispronounced both books' names, which was very common for all of us. "*Palms is really Psalms, with a silent p; and Job is really pronounced like Jobe.*"

Termite looked confused, and said, "That doesn't make any damn sense."

I agreed, and shrugged my shoulders. "*Sorry, man, that is just the way you are supposed to say the names. Honestly, brother, I have found dozens of names and places in the Bible that are very odd and weird. It is nearly impossible to pronounce about half of them. That's why I read the New Testament almost exclusively. The Old Testament, for the most part, doesn't make a whole lot of sense to me. Well, let me take that back. I do like reading the first few chapters of the first book, called Genesis, and I do like reading from the book you call Palms.*"

"OK, man, that's groovy." Termite changed the topic, "Hey, man, would you like to come to my place tonight for a Jesus happening?"

"*Sure, man, I'll be there. Can I bring my girlfriend?*"

"Of course. You can bring anyone you want."

When I arrived at the happening that night, people were playing guitars, beating on conga drums, and singing loudly. I did not know the person who appeared to be leading the happening. I asked Termite, "*Who is this guy?*"

"He is from a chapel in Costa Mesa, where supposedly the spirit is moving."

His answer caught me off guard. I asked, "*The spirit is moving! What in the hell is that supposed to mean?*"

He laughed and answered, "I was told that it is a spirit-filled chapel."

"*What is his name?*"

Termite paused, then replied, "I'm not sure, but I think his name is Robert. Robert something."

"*I'm cool with that. I'll call him Bobby.*"

I was impressed with Bobby's skill on the guitar, but his voice needed surgery. Everyone seemed to be having a good time. I could see a lot of white teeth and big smiles. He paused after a few songs and said, "I'm going to lead you into singing in the spirit."

I could not help myself; I blurted out, "*What in the hell is singing in the spirit?*"

I could tell by the expression on his face that I had somehow offended him. He gathered himself after an awkward pause, and responded, "Well, it is more of Jesus; and it is an expression of the Holy Spirit."

Story 4: Jesus Freaks

I responded immediately, "*Damn, I'm all in with the spirit stuff.*" I had no idea what the hell he was talking about, but I kind of felt sorry for him, because I think I had somehow hurt his feelings.

He started to gently fingerpick a melody on his guitar, then he began to sing softly in some strange language. A few others in the room joined in singing the weird sounding words with him. I did not have a clue what was going on, but I found it was kind of groovy. I thought, *This is so far-out. I dig this whacked-out, crazy stuff.*

Silently, and as inconspicuously as possible, I whispered the words, "*Spirit, if this is more of Jesus, bring it on.*" I opened my mouth, and started softly rambling some incoherent words. I was completely blown away by how amazing I felt. It was as if energy and love were flowing in and through me. I ever so cautiously commenced to make singing-like sounds.

I thought, *This is so groovy, what a trip.* And the best part is that I had no idea what was going on. It was definitely off the charts and into the wild blue yonder.

I turned to my left to see how my girlfriend was doing. She was not having a good time. She actually looked very uptight and angry.

I whispered in her ear, "*Are you all right?*"

She turned toward me and started to growl.

I freaked out! "*What's wrong with you?*"

She began to bark like a dog! I mean, she really barked like a dog, and bared her teeth as she growled.

Bobby saw what was going on with her and said, "Do not be afraid. This is a manifestation of a demon."

I thought, *Oh! Great, that really helps.*

He continued, "We can set her free from it in Jesus's name."

The strangest thought crossed my mind: *Oh my God, I've been dating a dog.* I tried to hold her hand as a sign of support, but she jerked away from me. I thought she was going to bite my face.

She jumped to her feet and headed for the front door. Bobby commanded the demon to stop, in Jesus's name. She stopped, turned toward him, and growled with bared teeth. He told the rest of us to just pray silently in the Spirit. I didn't know how to pray in the Spirit, so I just quietly asked God to help her.

The ordeal lasted for something like five minutes, with a lot of snarling and barking. Then, with a howl and scream, the demon left her. She cried for a while, and then she laughed, without any apparent embarrassment over what had just taken place in her life. She thanked us, and Jesus, for setting her free. No words can begin to describe my mixed emotions at that time.

That was just the beginning of seeing young people set free from all sorts of things, like drugs, intoxication, hate, racial prejudice, theft, vandalism, and other criminal acts that summer.

Unfortunately, many of the established churches didn't much like a bunch of hippies showing up at their church meetings. People started to call us Jesus freaks. Others said we were the beginning of what was later coined as the Jesus movement.

I wanted to check out Bobby's chapel. He told me he would be happy to pick me up and take me to their Sunday night meeting. I was cool with that, and I did go with him on Sunday night. To my delight and surprise, they met in a big circus tent. The music from their band was upbeat, and borderline rock and roll. I dug it.

A short, stout, balding man came to the microphone and welcomed all of us to the house of God. Most everyone chuckled at his reference to the circus tent being the house of God. Bobby leaned over and said, "That is Chuck Smith, the pastor of Calvary Chapel."

I liked him. Chuck's manner was laid-back and down-home charming. He was kind of like the loving, kind, cool uncle you never had.

Before Chuck got very far in teaching from the Bible, a wind started to blow. The wind got stronger and stronger by the minute. A long-haired hippie standing next to me said, "It is the wind of the Holy Spirit!"

I wasn't very confident about his observation. I suggested, *"Buddy, you might want to cut back on your pot smoking for a while."*

Story 4: Jesus Freaks

Then it happened. The wind blew so hard, the tent started to jerk and sway back and forth violently. Many of us headed for the exits. Just as I made it to safer ground a few feet outside the tent, the wind broke the tie-down lines. Within seconds, the tent lifted off the ground, and I could hear a loud cracking sound as some of the supporting wooden beams were snapped by the force of the wind. Then, suddenly, the tent collapsed in a massive heap. Everyone laughed and jumped around like a bunch of little kids jacked up on sugar and caffeine.

What appeared to be a disaster of a church meeting, turned out to be one of the best things that had ever happened to Calvary Chapel. The circus tent blowing down made it to the front page of the *Orange County Register* newspaper the very next day. Calvary Chapel was now on the map, began growing exponentially, and never did look back in the rearview mirror.

As spring turned into summer, my new friend Mario Murillo and I decided to go to the place with more hippies than anywhere else we knew of at the time. We headed north to Haight-Ashbury, and the University of California–Berkeley campus. I was eighteen, and Mario nineteen.

What I like to remember is that it was a season of faith and fun. We saw several unexplainable, groovy, far-out things happen back then, and they seemed to be the norm more than the exception, happening almost every day. Childlike, naïve faith was easy for a lot of us, because we didn't know any better. It was a wonderful season of celestial mystery and innocent love in action, when thousands of young people who wanted to know the truth found Jesus in the process.

The small group of Jesus freaks I met with in the spring of 1967 was about a couple dozen people. By the end of that summer, the group had grown to a few hundred. We used to say, "*The water is good, and the fishing is fine. Jump on in and see for yourself.*"

The pastor of one of the churches who had welcomed and loved all of us bought another church building in west Anaheim. He bought it because of the crazy growth of new young people gathering at his place. He asked Mario and me if we would start meeting with all these new young people. I asked, "*What does that mean, to meet with them?*"

He replied, "Well, Marty, it means that you would be the youth leaders at the new building."

I was more than a little blown away by his request. I was eighteen years old, and had been following Jesus for only a little more than three months. Mario didn't like the idea. He thought it would just tie us down, and prevent us from reaching out to other areas of California, especially Haight-Ashbury and the Berkeley campus.

However, a lot of groovy things were happening right at home in Orange County. At one of those early meetings, in the autumn of 1967 at Melodyland, which originally was a live theater-in-the-round right across the street from Disneyland, I met a very interesting, captivating speaker from New York.

The speaker was introduced to the crowd as a "real man of God." I thought that was a pretty strange title. I was one of the first hippie Jesus freaks he had ever met. He was the founder of Teen Challenge, and was personally introduced to me as Brother Dave. I was told that Teen Challenge was created to reach out to the hard-core drug addicts of New York City.

Well, Brother Dave was taken-up with me, and my enthusiasm for reaching out to other hippies. He asked if I would like to come to his private college in upstate New York. I really didn't know much about the college, so I asked, "*Brother Dave, what kind of college is it?*"

He kind of chuckled at my question, and said, "We study a lot of different topics at the college, but mainly the Bible. We prepare young people for the new life that is ahead of them."

He offered to raise the money for my airfare and all the tuition costs. This seemed too good to be true, but I knew the only way I would find out was by taking him up on his offer.

Story 5:
Unintended Consequences

Hurts and tormenting despair demand of us to give up,
Demanding our surrender in humiliating defeat.
Hope whispers there is life—don't give up
Look up! The Life Giver is near.
—Uncle Bear

Meeting David Wilkerson would radically change the direction of my life. The full scholarship sounded like a very cool idea. He had kindly and generously offered me a wonderful opportunity to obtain a college education, with a Bachelor of Divinity degree. I had never been to New York, and I did want to meet more Jesus people beyond California's borders. I had no idea at the time how short-lived my time at Brother Dave's college would be.

On New Year's Day of 1968, I flew to New York City with my friend Duck Dewy. Darrell Dewy was his actual birth name, but we called him Duck Dewy. He was the drummer in our rock 'n' roll garage band. Dewy was also invited by Brother Dave to come to his college, with a full scholarship.

I had never been to a city like New York before. We were given directions on how to get to the main Teen Challenge center in Brooklyn. From the airport, we had to ride three different subway trains. I tried to talk to people on the subways, but nobody would give me the time of day, let alone a conversation. I entertained myself by making sarcastic remarks to the other passengers, who completely and utterly ignored me. We finally got within walking distance of the center, located at 444 Clinton Avenue.

By the time we got there, it was night. The center had a high chain link fence all the way around it. At the entrance to the property was a gigantic gate that was securely locked. However, there was a sign high above us, on what appeared to be an intercom speaker, with some hand-written words on it, "Push the button and state your business." I thought, *Wow, that's real down-home friendly.*

I pushed the button several times before somebody finally spoke to us. "Hello, yeah, what do yah want? It's nighttime already. State your business."

For a couple of seconds I seriously regretted being there. But I thought, *What the hell did you expect, Marty, a welcoming party?*

After briefly interrogating us, the doorman yelled, "Yo!" "When you hear the buzzer, push the gate open, but don't let anybody else in wit' you. Only you and the Dewy guy are permitted to enter."

I replied sarcastically, "*There isn't anyone else wit' us.*"

"Good, let's keep it dat way." The buzzer screeched, and I pushed the huge gate open with a heave. The gate was spring-loaded, so when we let go of it, it slammed shut behind us with a bang.

When Duck Dewy and I finally got inside, the doorkeeper introduced himself to us. "Hey, I'm Stan. Anything you want, I'm your man."

"*OK, Stan the Man, that's great, because we just got here from California, and we don't know what room we are staying in.*"

Stan gestured with both hands palms up, about chest high, and said, "What? Do I look like a hotel clerk to you?"

"*No, I didn't think you were a hotel clerk, but you did offer to help us.*"

He shook his head back and forth and said, "Don't get cute wit' me."

"No, Stan, we meant no disrespect," Dewy answered.

"California, I never met anyone before from California."

Story 5: Unintended Consequences

Stan the Man smiled in a disturbing sort of way, and said, "Yah know dat God helps those who help themselves?"

I replied, *"No, Stan, I didn't know dat, but it does sound like a good idea."* I was beginning to think that Stan the Man was a bit unhinged from drug abuse, or maybe he was dropped on his head as a child. *"Stan, could you please tell us what to do or where to go?"*

He smiled again with that disturbing, kind of demented, expression and said, "Now we are getting somewhere. Brother John's office is all the way to the end of this hallway, on your right. You will see a sign that says Director's Office."

We were in luck. Brother John was in his office, and he welcomed us with a coherent discourse, and a nice touch of kindness in his demeanor. I was caught off guard, and surprised to discover that John was Brother Dave's actual biological brother. John personally saw us to our room, and made sure we were comfortable. John was a kind man, with a genuine love and heartfelt concern for the well-being of the recovering drug addicts at the center.

Dewy and I stayed at the Brooklyn Teen Challenge center for a couple of days, until we caught a ride with a couple of black brothers from New York City who were heading back to the school. They were both in their second year at the Bible college. They were really friendly and fun to be with, but the fun didn't last long.

The very first week at the college, it became apparent to me that it was going to be a long, cold winter. Asking questions had always been my mode of perceiving and learning, to better understand things. It had always been hard for me to just accept something being presented without questioning the premise of what was being taught, which never did go well in any of my High School classes.

Somehow, in some unexplainable way, we lost the art of classic critical thinking in the American culture of learning. The interaction of questions and answers between teacher and student always seemed to me the best way to learn—and especially to learn how to think, not just memorize spoon-fed concepts or beliefs. However, I quickly learned that this college was very similar to the public schools I had attended. They just didn't put much emphasis or value on questions from students. For some strange reason, they thought just about any question asked regarding what they were teaching was a challenge to their authority or credibility.

I tried to get with the program at the college, despite their dogmatic approach. I actually got straight A's my first semester. However, I was beginning to develop a bad attitude, and a bit of resentment toward some of my teachers. I got along fairly well with all the students. I wasn't trying to be trouble or cause any turmoil. I was just unable to go along with the "swallow anything that is served up as sound doctrine routine."

I really could not see the trees for the forest. Unbeknown to me, I had torn loose my mooring lines, and was drifting into uncharted waters. The isolation syndrome of a bad attitude and the manure of my deep-seated resentment against authority, were pulling me downward into the undertow of a gnarly wipeout.

I did not know it at the time, because being deceived usually means you are clueless as to what is happening, even if it is happening right in front of your nose. All I knew was that I was right, and they were wrong.

Whenever I was given a test on some aspect of theology, typology, eschatology, or any other ology, I would write down the answer they wanted to hear, and then I would write down my answer next to it. The practice of dual answering didn't go over very well with my instructors. The teaching staff was not entertained.

One of my "ology" instructors called me aside to give me a warning:

"Your rebellious posturing and general lack of respect shown to the school staff has given us no choice but to give you an ultimatum: either shape-up, or be prepared to lose your scholarship and be shipped-out."

"*Rebellious! Who are you to call me rebellious?*"

"Marty, I am your friend, and I am an elder in your life at this school."

Story 5: Unintended Consequences

"*Oh! So, now you are an elder in my life? I thought you were my friend and teacher, but now you are my elder. I know what elder means. It is a code word for being an uptight religious legalist.*"

"Now Marty, guard your tongue, young man."

"*Guard my tongue? Guard my tongue! Who in the hell do you think you are?*"

"Marty, please stop and take a look at yourself. You are inadvertently becoming an un-submissive rebel without a cause."

"*Do you really expect me to submit to your religious determinism? If taking a stand against your dictatorial rule makes me a rebel, then yes, I am proud to be a rebel without a cause.*"

I was certain that I was right and they were wrong. I had unadvisedly become ensnared by an attitude of self-righteousness regarding their path of spiritual instruction. I had caught the disease. I had eaten of the forbidden fruit from the tree of the knowledge of good and evil. I was now judging them for their judging me! I knew Jesus had said I was not to be a judge, or I would be judged in like manner, but I had fallen into the trap, and now it had me in its destructive grip. Soon, I would be living out, the fruit of a toxic unintended consequence.

I became resentful and very uptight. One thing led to another, and I left the college halfway through my second year. My heart had grown cold, and my relationship with Christ had all but vanished. I was in full-on rebellion against organized religion. I called it "churchy-anity." I really can't say that I backslid. It was more like I took a back-dive.

Story 6:
Everything Had Changed

I've been told that someday your life will flash before you
I do hope it's worth watching.
—Uncle Bear

When I returned to Anaheim, everything was strangely different. Everyone seemed to have changed a great deal since I had left. I felt out of place. This was my hometown, but I no longer fit into the scenery. All my old friends appeared awkwardly uncomfortable around me.

It didn't take me long to realize that it was me who had been doing all the changing. I couldn't hang out with old friends and party without feeling oddly guilty. And I couldn't take off in my El Camino truck and go to the beach—my parents had sold my truck while I was at college.

I felt completely ripped off. My friends who had met Jesus looked at me like I had some kind of disease or something. Mainly, it was because I had returned from college with a really rotten attitude. I was extremely disinterested in "churchy-anity," or any church-related activity. I now found it all so boring.

I was not the same person I used to be. Rusty, one of the first friends I had led to Jesus mentioned that I should read some C. S. Lewis book called *The Four Loves*. He said the book was cool, and that I could possibly discover my shadow self, and thereby be able to discover my true

Story 6: Everything Had Changed

self. I told him I would get right on it. I lied! All I knew was that it was no longer fun or far-out for me to follow the path of God.

I had been a Jesus freak. I briefly went to Bible College, and now I abhorred organized religion. I blamed the college for ruining my walk with Jesus. I found the blame game really easy to play, and became pretty good at it. I guess anyone could, with enough practice. The rules are very simple. You simply blame someone else for your shortcomings, failures, bad habits, bad breath—anything you want.

I learned along the way, unfortunately, that some poor souls play the blame game all the time, maybe even to their dying day. Of course, it goes without saying that most North Americans live in mass denial of death, anyway. I had pretty much lost my way and the meaning of life.

I had to do something. I was becoming claustrophobic. I needed to escape into a new movie with all new characters. It took me about ten minutes to come up with a foolproof plan. Well, at least I got the *fool* part down fairly well. It's amazing how little time it can take to come up with a very ill-advised plan for your life. It was my time to conquer the world, and make my mark in antiquity.

At the time, I had no idea that the consequences of my ill-conceived plan would lead me to committing various crimes, facing life and death situations, and becoming a fugitive on the run from the FBI.

I would go back to the place where I was born, Rock Island, Illinois. I had not lived there since I was five years old. I could stay with my dear grandmother, and I could start my college career all over again. Of course, I could not qualify for any state university to begin with, but I could get into the local community college.

Two weeks later, I was on a plane headed for Chicago. Once in the Windy City, I transferred to a Greyhound bus headed for Rock Island, Illinois. One week later, I was enrolled in Black Hawk Community College.

During the first week of classes, I made some new friends. We had a lot of personal freedom at this college. It was not unusual to see a student light up a joint and pass it around in the college lunchroom or the courtyard area.

I bought a 1949 candy apple red International Harvester truck with the money I had saved while working at a gas station when I was sixteen. I called it my *soul* truck, because it was born the same year I was born. It made good hippie sense to me at the time to have my own soul truck.

I had a lot of stored-up youthful energy in those days, and found a few ways to release all that bottled-up juice and enthusiasm. Within a few months, I had founded a nonprofit corporation, and started an underground newspaper, a donation-only coffeehouse, and the beginnings of a cultural arts center. All of which were located at the previously owed Celebrity Nightclub.

By the time spring rolled around, a producer at the local TV station asked if I would like to have my own twelve-week summer TV show. The TV station thought this would be a good public relations service. They had no idea how wrong they were. There were twelve shows in all, each one a half hour long, shown on Wednesday mornings, and again on Wednesday evenings.

I didn't know the first thing about running an educational TV show. All I knew how to do was intuitively entertain people. I had a different local band or musician play at each taping, and I always made sure I had a politically contentious person or some radical hippie onboard to interview.

The show caused a lot of controversy. I was told it was actually getting really good eyeballs, which meant, to the TV station's surprise, a lot of people were actually watching the show. The producer told me I was developing what he called a cult following.

I was more surprised than anyone that people were actually watching the show. I was just being kind of outrageous, and trying to have some offbeat fun with it. I never did take it seriously. I kind of thought

Story 6: Everything Had Changed

I might have a shot at being the next Chuck Barris, of the *Gong Show* television fame.

The TV station wanted to continue the show in their fall lineup, but the sponsors thought the show and I were too controversial. It did not continue.

Newspaper clip at Celebrity Night Club with Marty & Rev. Ron

Story 7:
Light Up My Life

*I had contracted a disease that affects the brain
of a great many young people.
I was bored out of my mind!*
—Uncle Bear

After my TV show was finished, I was not at all interested in going back to college in the fall, and the scene in Rock Island, Illinois, and its sister city, Davenport, Iowa, was not the most exciting in the world. The two cities were separated only by water—the Mighty Mississippi River, that is.

I received a phone call from two of my lifelong friends, Wild Will and Billy Beans. Beans had a serious problem with excess gas. Will and Billy had started a candle company, and wanted me to join as a full partner. They had rented an old warehouse in a small town called Running Springs, in the mountains of Southern California, on the main road to Big Bear City.

It took me about an hour to call them back and tell them I would be seeing them in a few days. I booked a flight, and said good-bye to my friends in the Midwest. I flew into LAX, caught one of the hourly buses to Disneyland, and stayed with my parents for a couple of days in Anaheim.

Wild Will drove down from the mountains to say hi to his parents and pick me up at mine. Will was a Jesus freak for a few months, but it

Story 7: Light Up My Life

didn't last. Rock and roll was his true god. It was really good to see an old friend. There's just something about being childhood friends that seems to bond you for life. I don't know why.

As we drove to the mountains, we talked and got caught up with each other's lives. We talked for a little while about the candle business, but then we smoked a pipe-full of hashish, and finished it off with a cold beer from his VW bus's ice-box.

"Marty, would you like to know where I got such kick-ass hash?" he asked.

I tried to speak, but all I could do was nod my head and say, "*Yeah.*"

"Well, brother, do you remember Farmer John Griggs, the founder of the Brotherhood of Eternal Love?"

"*Yes, of course. We grew up together in the same neighborhood.*"

"Well, my man, Farmer John and a few other guys from the Brotherhood took a trip to Afghanistan, where they scored something like one thousand pounds of black, hand-pounded, top-grade hashish."

"*Whoa, that's a lot of hash. How did they get that much hashish back to the States?*"

"That, my friend, is exactly the right question. They smuggled it into India, and delivered it to Goa, on the southwest coast of India."

"*Why Goa?*" I asked.

"Goa is where they specialize in building handmade sailboats," answered Will.

"*No way!*"

"Yes way!"

Wild Will continued to tell the story, while I reached for another beer. "They had a sailboat custom built for them."

"*Why?*" I asked.

"So they could stash a half ton of Afghan black hashish, pounded into the keel of the sailboat." With that proclamation, Wild Will laughed out loud like a crazy, drunken cowboy.

After a few minutes of stoned laughter, Will gathered himself back together and continued, "They hired a crew to help them sail it back to Maui, Hawaii."

"*Why Maui and not California?*" I asked.

"Because the Brotherhood owns land in Maui, and the Coast Guard in Hawaii is really laid-back. The Coast Guard is used to seeing rich people sailing their hundred-foot sailboats from island to island."

"*Wouldn't flying an Indian flag of registration cause some curiosity?*"

"That is exactly why they had it registered in Malta."

"*Why Malta?*"

"Good question. Malta is a very neutral country, and thousands of private sailboats, yachts, and commercial vessels are registered there. That's exactly why we wanted you to join us on our way to freedom."

"*I don't understand—what do you mean by freedom?*"

"Money, dude! And I mean a whole lot of money. We can become millionaires, and Marty, you have the brains that can bring it all together for us."

"*Brains! Damn, Will, I don't have a clue what you are talking about, and I'm the brain who is going to make this happen?*"

"OK, OK, you're right. I got way too spaced-out with my head trip."

I agreed, and asked him to just finish telling me what had happened with the Brotherhood.

"From Hawaii, they smuggled back smaller quantities in suitcases. They sold nine hundred pounds for fifteen hundred dollars per pound. They sold everything in a few weeks, from the Mystic Arts head shop in Laguna Beach. They pocketed over a million dollars, and still had one hundred pounds of personal stash."

"*What are they doing now?*"

"Good question! Farmer John is still dealing big time. He spends his time between his pad in Laguna Canyon, the lakeside ranch in Idyllwild,

Story 7: Light Up My Life

and his farm in Maui. Two of the other dudes from the Brotherhood went north, and bought a very cool place to live in Oregon."

"*Where in Oregon?*" I asked.

"They bought a piece of prime property and a big kick-butt cabin on the Rouge River, near the town of Cave Junction. We plan on visiting them in the spring."

"*What do you mean, visiting them in the spring? I thought we were going to be running a candle company.*"

"Yeah, man, we will be doing the candle thing all winter long in the mountains, but in the spring, we head north. We will be on the highway to freedom."

"*Will, what the hell are you talking about?*"

"We are going to visit our rich Brotherhood friends in Cave Junction, on our way to Canada."

"*Canada! Why would we be doing that if we have a successful candle company?*"

"Because the candles are small time, and we are on the open road, headed for the Promise-land."

"*Will, you are blowing my mind. I didn't come back here to fly off to Afghanistan!*"

"No, man, we aren't flying off to Afghanistan. We will be driving to BC, Canada, after leaving Cave Junction."

"*British Columbia?*"

"Yeah, man, BC. British Columbia, Canada."

I was beginning to get angry at the overwhelming confusion of Wild Will's spaced-out explanation. "*Why in the hell would we be headed for BC?*"

"OK, Marty, take it easy, everything is cool. We knew you could help us run a successful candle company, but we knew you were bigger than that. You are the perfect head to help us run a forty-acre marijuana plantation."

"*You have got to be putting me on!*"

"No, man, trust me, it's for real, and it's our E-ticket to the whole wide world. After we harvest the forty acres of marijuana and sell it back in Southern California, we will have enough money to do the sailboat deal with Afghan hash and our own sailboat from Goa, India. We are going to be rich, and we will be free to sail the seven seas."

Story 8:
Forty Acres of Marijuana

*I learned the old-fashioned way, by experience,
that sowing is a lot easier than reaping.*
—Uncle Bear

The candle company did do well that winter. We only sold assorted dozens of twelve-inch-high candles. We pretty much had the head shop business wired in Southern California. We had actually landed a deal with May Company of California, known to most as The May Co. For their first order, they wanted a gross order of candles per store for ten of their department stores in California. We did the math. Ten stores times one hundred forty-four candles per store equaled 1,440 candles, first order!

The three of us talked it over at great length. Our conclusion was that we would no longer own the candle business, but in function and fact, the candle company would own us. If we had used our common sense, I think we could have made a small fortune within a few years with the candle business.

However, when you are twenty years old, days, weeks, and maybe months, are about as far out as you can think toward any future event. Shortsightedness plagues many a young person, and for some it doesn't seem to ever get much better; as the years go by, a strange sort of overall blindness seems to set in on the soul and the spirit.

Acquiring wealth—or getting ahead in life—for a young person, is generally perceived as a positive in our modern culture. Unfortunately, opportunities come more often than not in the form of a get-rich-quick scheme of some sort that usually leaves the individual disappointed, discouraged, and delusional; and in some cases behind bars.

Spring did come early that year, and we—Wild Will, Billy Beans, and Marty Berry—were off to meet up with some of our Brotherhood of Eternal Love friends in Cave Junction, Oregon. They fronted us marijuana seeds that they claimed were from some awesome hybrid stock in Mexico. They said the seeds were the same ones being planted in Maui by none other than Farmer John Griggs, and he was calling the crop Maui Wowi.

Marty & watchdog at Cave Junction, Oregon

Story 8: Forty Acres of Marijuana

We smoked hashish with our extended family of the Brotherhood until the early hours of the morning. I only vaguely remember going to sleep. However, I do remember waking up to a strange, bizarre sensation. One of their watchdogs was licking my face. I had somehow ended up sleeping on the wooden planks of the front porch, with a bag of brown rice as my pillow.

We didn't continue our journey north to Canada until noon the next day. Because of our late start, we crossed the border into Canada early the next morning. It was my twenty-first birthday the day we entered Canada.

After driving on what felt like an endless narrow road of mountain curves, we came to the Slocan River. We were now on the last leg of our trip. We were getting closer to the road sign that would eventually turn into a dirt road taking us to our forty-acre would-be marijuana plantation.

We made a couple of wrong turns, but eventually found the right road. It was a very untraveled dirt road no more than two ruts that vaguely looked like tire tracks. After a few miles on the dirt road, we came to the locked gate we were looking for.

An unmistakable greeting was carved into the huge timber pole securing the gate: "Enter at your own risk! Occupant is trigger-happy!" It took us a few minutes to remember where the key to the padlock was hidden under a nearby granite rock.

After opening the gate, we ran across a grassy field like a bunch of kids at summer camp. We ran with abandonment toward the only structure on the property, a dilapidated old shack.

Without warning, to our startled complete surprise and utter shock, a black bear was running toward us from about forty yards away, and closing. I reacted like a crazed madman jacked up on adrenaline. I bolted toward the bear with the raw instinct of an Apache Indian warrior. I yelled, screamed, and shouted obscenities as I ran at the bear with all my might. When I was only a few yards from the black bear, with a howling roar, it turned to the left and ran toward the nearby woods.

With exuberant hoots and hollers, they congratulated me on my complete and utter insanity.

Will asked, "What in the hell were you thinking?"

"*That's just it. I wasn't thinking. I just reacted without thinking.*"

Billy fell backward into the tall grass, laughing so hard that I could not understand what he was trying to say.

Finally, he became somewhat coherent. "Bear! Marty, you are the bear. You are the Bear!"

After our emotions calmed down and the laughter had ceased, we walked over to the only known convenience, if you could call it that. It was a one-room shack, about fifteen feet by twenty feet. It had an old wood stove, a few rusty pots and pans hanging on the wall, and a three-legged table with two chairs. The windows had all been broken out, years ago by the looks of the inside of the cabin.

We discovered during our first night in the shack that the roof had more than a few leaks, given the amount of rain that poured through. The next night, one of us slept in the shack and the other two spent the night in the van.

We built a huge campfire next to the Slocan River. It was easy to find the right size of round river rocks to encircle our fire pit. We were very pleased with our effort. We even found some old logs that made for good seating around the campfire.

Wild Will was really into some Native Indian rituals. He kind of saw himself as a hippie medicine man. As long as it was just plain, stupid fun, such as dancing around the campfire at night and making up our own version of Native American chanting, I was cool with that. However, he did get a little on the weird side of the American Indian spirit stuff.

When Will started going into this pagan/oneness thing—like brother tree and sister flower, with a little bit of "Let's all become one mind and one spirit with nature"—it was no longer fun, and got kind of creepy. He started interpreting the signs and omens of the wind, water, and moon. Billy and I told Will to tone down the weirdness channel for the time being—at least until we had our cash crop in and growing.

Story 8: Forty Acres of Marijuana

After spending a couple of days surveying the land, we decided to get on with planting our seeds. Every marijuana seed was hand planted, and we had to make sure our plantings were discreet. We wanted the marijuana plants to blend in with the natural terrain.

The ground was pretty moist from all the spring rain, making it easy to dig those little holes in which each marijuana seed was planted. We then covered each seed with about a half inch of wet soil.

To our surprise, it took us less than a month to plant the entire forty acres. Now, granted, we were cautious in the way we planted, so not every square foot of the forty acres had marijuana plants. We did not want to get busted by some Canadian Mountie passing over in a small aircraft.

The property didn't even have an outhouse. So every time we needed to do our business, we had to make sure we took a shovel along. In a kind of weird way, I felt like a Boy Scout—maybe because I had been thrown out of the Cub Scouts.

Story 9:
Got Milk?

*Fences on a marijuana farm need to be cow high,
pig tight, and electrified if possible.*
—Uncle Bear

Almost all the marijuana seeds had germinated and sprouted, reaching for life and kissing the sky. I was amazed at how fast the crop was shooting upward, all over the forty acres. Maybe that's one reason it's called weed; it sure did grow like a weed.

We believed that music had a special vibe, and could increase the volume and potency of our crop. We had with us a tiny generator that could recharge our extra car battery, which we hooked up to an old eight-track cassette tape player salvaged from somebody's trashed car. We played Hendrix, the Doors, Bread, the Beatles, the Moody Blues and Crosby, Stills, Nash, and Young most of the time. The marijuana seemed to love the vibe of the music. Well, at least *we* did.

On one particularly beautiful afternoon, I had finished my morning watering of the marijuana plants. It looked like a perfect day to take a walk in the natural surroundings by myself. I walked aimlessly along the river for well over an hour without seeing another soul. I began to sing spontaneously, first in English, and then in what I call my spirit voice.

A peaceful, romantic urge came upon me as I observed the richness of the vivid shades of green all around me. I sat comfortably

Story 9: Got Milk?

under the massive limbs of a sugar pine and pondered the beauty of my surroundings for several minutes, until time seemed to vanish. Words effortlessly flowed into my conscious thoughts, and the words became poetry. I always tried to carry my little leather-bound journal with me. These are the words I put to paper on that sunny, wonder-filled day.

> *Green, glorious green was everywhere to be seen,*
> *The morning sun danced and shone with brilliance gleaned,*
> *Reverberating through the royal forest sheen,*
> *The proud pine, noble fir, and giant cedars leaned,*
> *Reaching for the sky whispering green, glorious serene,*
> *Leaves of the mighty oak and the timid aspen calling me,*
> *The untold shades of green surrounded me with glee,*
> *Green, glorious green was everywhere to be seen.*

Every morning, we watered the marijuana plants by hand from the waters of the Slocan River. Many an afternoon we would sit on the banks of the river, cooling our heels in the cold water or hand-washing our clothes. We were pleased to have some neighbors across the river from us. These neighbors were a small herd of dairy cows. Watching them was kind of peaceful. Every day, late in the afternoon, they would go back home, disappearing over the nearby grassy hill.

One day toward the end of June, we happened to notice that the river was getting lower. It was actually getting lower almost every day. The spring snowmelt was slowing down. We began to wonder just how low this once-roaring river was going to get for its final summer level. One week later, all of us agreed that it looked as though the river had found its final summer stage, or at least we hoped it wouldn't go any lower.

One of the dairy cows seemed to agree with us, because she made her way across the river to our side. We laughed with amusement, and greeted our new friend with cheers of delight. I named the cow Moo-nah, the Milk Machine. We actually talked about how we might be able to milk Moo-nah. We finally decided to let her be, and just enjoy her company. However, she did outlive her welcome very quickly.

The next day, Moo-nah brought two friends with her as she crossed to our side of the river. We were entertained by having three of them join us. But the next day, five of the cows crossed over, and they started to graze, as is the custom of dairy cows.

One of Moo-nah's friends started munching on some of our precious marijuana crop. All three of us jumped to our feet, screaming at the cows, and herding them back to the other side of the river. But it was too late; one of them had tasted marijuana.

I don't know how cows communicate with each other, but somehow they do. The next day, we had a dozen hungry cows making their way across the river. They didn't waste any time—all twelve went straight for the marijuana plants.

It was now war! They were the invaders, and we were defenders of the land. After all, we did pay $150 to lease the land for one year. At first, we tried to defend our turf in a civil manner by shooing the cows back across the river, but that didn't last long.

It looked like the dairy cows were committed to eating our marijuana crop. We met around the campfire to discuss our options, and decided to build a makeshift fence along the river where the bovines were crossing.

Within the week, the entire herd of some twenty-eight dairy cows were crossing the river every day. We did build a fence along the riverbank in hopes it would divert the cows downstream. But it was no use. The cows would just go around it, and amble their way back upstream to the marijuana.

We reinforced the fence as best we could, and then stood guard at each end of it. It didn't matter if we hit the cows with a branch or small limb from a nearby tree. I am ashamed to admit that I hit more than one of those cows as hard as I could on their thick skulls, but to no

Story 9: Got Milk?

avail. It was too late. The cows would rather die than switch. They were hooked on marijuana, and wanted more. Nothing could stop them now; they just kept on coming. They even got tired of going around the fence, so they started tearing the fence apart with their thick heads, massive bodies and huge hooves.

We were defeated; the cows had won. Finally, one of the neighbors downriver from us dropped by to see how we were doing. He was an American draft dodger living in BC. We had already eaten dinner, and were smoking some weed while we sat around the campfire. He smiled broadly when we told him of our defeat.

Laughing out loud he said, "Those dairy cows have been crossing over to this side of the river every year for God knows how many years. It is part of their rite of passage every year after the spring runoff." Still laughing, he added, "Nobody told them that you had leased the land."

We were not only defeated, but now we were also humiliated, by a herd of dairy cows. What in the world were we going to do?

We sat around the campfire for hours that night, trying to make sense of our defeat. When everything was said and done about the condition of our marijuana crop, we began to laugh at our stupidity and general lack of knowledge about how to grow anything. We laughed and laughed, until a total silence came over us. We sat by the fire until the early hours of the morning. We had consumed a great deal of wine.

Break on Through to the Other Side

Friends with Marty until they ate his marijuana

Story 10:
On the Road Again

*When you throw your cares to the wind,
you just might want to check and see
which way the wind is blowing.*
—Uncle Bear

Leaving the forty acres and our marijuana crop, humiliated at being defeated by a gang of dairy cows, was a hard lump of curd to swallow. Will wanted to call our friends in the Brotherhood back in Laguna Beach. However, Beans and I were too "embare-assed" to call them. So we decided to take a road trip all the way across Canada to Nova Scotia!

When you make mistakes and don't know what to do, you might as well do something that makes no sense whatsoever. And that is exactly what we did. I think our new nicknames could have been Stupid, Stupider, and Stupidest.

We were young and threw care to the wind. The only problem was the wind didn't care where we threw anything. We were on our own, and headed in the wrong direction. We pooled all our money together, and lived like there was no tomorrow.

We did pull up all the remaining marijuana plants out of the ground before we left. So we smoked dope and drove each day until the sun went down. Then we would pull the van over, smoke some more pot, and crash for the night. We were not in any hurry, so we really didn't care how many miles a day we drove.

When we finally reached Nova Scotia, we were down to our last dollars. We had smoked all the pot we had harvested from the forty acres. We didn't have a clue what to do next. One thing was certain the world was not going to be conquered by the likes of us. So we split up. I took off on my own after a minor disagreement with the other two, and hitchhiked to the closest place I could think of where I knew I could crash at a friend's place. *Rock Island, Illinois, here I come, ready or not.* "Not!" would have been a much better answer.

On my way to Rock Island, I stopped by a friend's frat house at the University of Chicago. The hippies in the house seemed to be up in arms about something that had happened. I asked my friend, *"Dude, why is everyone so uptight?"*

"Do you remember the Demon-crats National Convention here in the Windy City, and the Chicago Seven brothers who were arrested?"

"Yes, of course I remember."

"Did you know they were all sentenced to five years in prison, and in addition to that, they were each fined five thousand dollars?"

"No, I'm sorry. I did not know that."

"Did you know that nine students were shot at Kent State by our National Guard during a peaceful anti-Vietnam rally, and that four of them died?"

I was ashamed to answer, *"Yeah, I heard about it."*

"You heard about it! Where in the hell have you been, Marty?"

"Uh, well, British Columbia to Nova Scotia, and everywhere in between."

"Are you for real, man?"

I hesitated, then I spoke. *"Not really, I kind of dropped out of current events in the United States, and I've been on the road for the last few weeks."*

"Dude, you need to get your act together and get plugged into what is happening in this messed-up country of ours."

"Yeah, man, you're right—I have no excuse."

Story 10: On the Road Again

The next morning, I was awakened by a gentle, mysterious voice. "Marty, Marty, it's time to get up. Wake up, handsome."

I opened my eyes, and at first glance wondered if I was dreaming. I had never heard such a rhythmic voice, nor seen this enchanting face before. She was more than pretty. She was dazzling, with her ravishing red hair and dark lavender-blue eyes. Before I could think, I asked, "*Are you Irish?*"

"No, I'm an American with a Russian family tree. Is that OK?"

"*Yes, of course it is all right. You are the first Russian I've ever met. What is your name?*"

"They call me Misty."

"*They call you Misty. Is that your real name?*"

"My real name is Misery!"

I laughed so hard, I nearly lost control of my bladder. "*No, truthfully, what is your real name?*"

"Wouldn't you like to know."

"*Yes, I really would like to know.*"

"If Misty isn't good enough for you, I will be having breakfast with someone else."

I didn't ask her again what her name really was. We became immediate friends. She was like no other girl I had ever met. Her manner was alluring and sensuous. Yet, at other times, she had a catlike trait of avoidance, shunning my affection. However, Misty had a cryptic way of soothing my guilty conscience, overshadowing my bad memories of failure and guilt. During the first few days I was with her, it was as if there wasn't a problem in the world.

Unfortunately, the repose of serenity didn't last long. Soon thereafter, Misty marched into the room, looking like she was on a mission. "Jerry Rubin and Abby Hoffman both told me that you were one of the golden boys."

"*Golden boys! What is that supposed to mean?*"

"They said you could be one of the key players in the new Students for a Democratic Society."

"*Misty, that's really weird. Jerry and Abby didn't even like the leaders of the SDS.*"

"Marty that is exactly why they wanted to see you regroup and restart the SDS." The volume of her voice rose a few decibels. "They are leaderless! It is the perfect time to rally the old guard."

"*Misty, please understand. I have been a friend of the Students for a Democratic Society in Chicago and in Iowa City, but I never saw myself as any kind of leader.*"

"Marty, I think it would be so cool if you were the leader of the new student movement and a new SDS. They need a real leader who will rally them to action." As I thought about what she had just said, she quickly added a very specific request, "If we could just figure out a way to help the student movement, but also help ourselves in the process."

Her suggestion puzzled me. "*What do you mean by help ourselves?*"

"It would be great, Marty, for you to be the leader of the rejuvenated SDS. But when it's all said and done, we need to figure out how to make a lot of money."

"*How much is a lot of money?*"

She smirked and replied, "We need to first set some financial goals. We need to make ten thousand dollars, then one hundred thousand dollars, and finally, one million dollars."

I tried to keep my composure. "*Wow, that sounds oddly familiar.*"

She was visibly upset by my response. She snapped back at me with a blistering question, "What's odd about making a lot of money? What's odd about making a million dollars?"

My conscious thoughts were clouded by my desire to have her. I agreed with her that there must be some way to accomplish both endeavors—helping the student movement and making a dump load of money.

"Marty, it's time for us to partner up and increase our potential exponentially," she said.

That sounded pretty far-out, and it meant we would be together. I wondered if she was my soul mate. I hoped she was, and I wanted to

Story 10: On the Road Again

please her like no other girl I had met before. I felt as if I would do almost anything to win her over. She was exotic and enchanting. Her alluring manner held me captivated. She was undeniably mesmerizing.

When I shared my feelings with her, she laughed with a strange sort of glee. Her expression softened into a smile reminiscent of the Mona Lisa. She leaned toward me and looked directly into my eyes with those enchanting dark lavender-blue eyes. Now, only a few inches from my face, she gently coaxed me with these words, "Do you really think you can give me the kind of life that I need, that I deserve?"

Without thinking I replied, "*Yes! I can.*"

She paused, smiled mischievously, and asked, "What will you do for me, Marty?"

"*I will do whatever it takes.*"

"Really? Whatever it takes?"

I felt uncomfortably awkward, and a bit daunted, but I assured her, "*Yes, I can do it. Whatever it takes, I will do it.*"

She put the Mona Lisa smile back on and replied, "Time will tell whether you are a very gifted boy, or a man who can take care of me."

I was only twenty-one, by three months, but I thought I was a man. I knew I had to prove to her and myself that I was, in fact, a man.

After only a couple of weeks of intoxicating romance, it was time for me to make plans and get busy. All my best contacts were in Rock Island. I wondered if my best friend was still there, and if I could hang my beret at his place for a few weeks. I used the phone at the frat house. "*Yo Mark! It's Marty.*"

"Hey, Marty, how are yah do'n?"

"*Well, it's been a total bummer of a summer so far, but it's all about to change.*"

"Brother, you know you are welcome here at my place any time, and for as long as you want."

"*Thanks, Mark. I really do appreciate the offer, and I'm going to take you up on it.*"

When I told Misty that I was headed to Rock Island, she asked me how much money I had. Through my embarrassment, I told her the truth.

"*Misty, I only have a few bucks to my name.*"

"Unfortunately, that is exactly what I thought you would say, and that is why I'm going to Miami."

"*Why are you going to Miami?*"

"My rich grandmother lives there, and I am her favorite granddaughter. She has already said on the phone that she will lend me one thousand dollars for a project I'm working on for college. When you get to Rock Island, open a bank account, and I will wire you a thousand dollars."

"*Wow, what can I say?*"

"You can say thank you."

"*Thank you! Thank you! Thank you!*"

"Marty, this means that you had better get your act together, and live up to my expectations."

"*I will do my best.*"

"I'm not interested in your best. I'm only interested in results, and where I'm going to be in the future. I hope you don't disappoint me."

"*All I need is a chance to prove myself, and I will not disappoint you.*"

The next morning, I hitchhiked to Rock Island, arriving by early afternoon. It was a short walk over to Mark's pad from where I had been dropped off by my last ride. He was thoroughly stoned and drunk when I got there. So basically nothing had changed in the last year.

One thousand dollars was wired to me from Miami. Mark told me about a dealer friend of his in Amsterdam, with whom he had done a couple of deals. He would send this Dutch dealer five hundred dollars, and then, in a couple of weeks, receive a box of Dutch chocolate with a pound of Afghan hashish hidden in the chocolates. We could sell the hash by the ounce and by the gram. We would more than quadruple our money within the month.

Story 10: On the Road Again

I told Mark I was willing to invest a thousand dollars to get things moving. I had already done the math in my head. I figured it would take only two shipments of Afghan hash to reach the first goal of ten thousand dollars.

We sent off a $1,000 money order to our would-be Dutch friend in Amsterdam. All we had to do was sit back and wait for the chocolates to come in the mail. We got high, stoned, and drunk for days on end while we waited for the chocolates to arrive. Two weeks went by, and no package had come in the mail. Mark assured me that everything was OK, and not to worry. He had phoned his Dutch friend, who said the chocolates were in the mail.

The third week went by, and no package arrived. I was beginning to panic. Mark called the Dutch dealer on the phone, but there was no answer. We called every day, until there was a recorded message in both Dutch and English from the telephone company. The message was clear. The phone number we were calling had been disconnected. We sent letters in the mail every day for two weeks, but never received a response. Finally, one of our letters was sent back from Holland, saying basically no one by that name still lived at that address. Either we had been ripped off, or he had been arrested.

I was confused and angry that my hippie dream had vanished into thin air twice in the same year. I felt like my life was out of control. I was in a downward spiral, with no bottom in sight. Resentment and outright bitterness at everything began to fester in my soul. I desperately wanted to feel free, but I was trapped in a self-imposed cage of failure. I was embarrassed and humiliated, but I knew I had to call Misty and tell her the bad news.

To my complete shock, Misty's reaction to the bad news was way off the Richter scale. She ripped me up one side, and then down the other. The bottom line of our conversation was basically that I needed to do whatever was necessary to get her thousand dollars back, and if I ever thought I would see her again, it had better happen sooner rather than later.

My heart was becoming cold and hard. I blamed the government, the cops, society, the Vietnam War—anybody and everybody except myself. Anger and rage were festering in me like a decaying laceration. All kinds of strange stuff began to ignite in my head as I continually replayed the bad memories and events of my life.

The university students at Kent State being shot and killed by the National Guard became an obsession. I covered the walls of Mark's pad with headline newspaper photos of the Kent State massacre, and of wounded and dead US soldiers from the Vietnam War. I put up posters of militant student leaders, the Chicago Seven, and the Weather Underground, as well as posters of controversial musicians such as the Doors, Jimi Hendrix, and Janis Joplin. I read Jerry Rubin's book, *DO IT!*

Paranoia burst to the surface, and my seething anger was channeled into all-out retaliation against the establishment and the government. It was time to arm ourselves and devise a plan, and that was exactly what I thought we were going to do. I just didn't have a plan yet.

Somehow, we had convinced ourselves that we needed to be on a crusade against the evil empire. It's amazing what drugs and staying half-drunk for weeks on end can do to your perception of reality.

Story 11:
Drugs & Guns

*The mind of a human being is fearfully and wonderfully made,
with complex instinctive powers that enable us to believe
whatever we want to believe, against all reason,
all common sense, and all odds.*
—Uncle Bear

Mark and I scratched together enough money from local friends and family to buy a kilo of weed. We thought it would be a good way to have some smoke, and be able to sell the rest to make a little money while we figured out what we were going to do.

The problem was we sold only a few ounces of the marijuana. We took most of the proceeds and went shopping for some food, and a lot of beer and wine. We felt fortunate to discover a sale on gallon bottles of red wine. We ended up buying four gallons of the cheap wine and a case of Blue Ribbon beer from Milwaukee, but we almost forgot to buy any food.

We had a daily ritual of smoking dope, drinking red wine, and munching away, mainly on snack food crap. We were definitely getting more paranoid by the day. Repeatedly, Mark would declare, "After all, they shot us first!" I would enthusiastically reply, "*And what the hell are we going to do about it?*"

We talked a lot about vindicating the deaths of our brothers and sisters at Kent State. Our seething rhetoric went on for days on end—until one night we dropped some LSD, and began to plan how we could wake this country up and turn it around.

After staying up all night tripping on acid and strategizing, Mark and I came up with a plan. We decided the best way to do this was to become like the James Gang, only with the style of Robin Hood.

We would start robbing banks. The money in the banks was insured—which guaranteed that the common folk wouldn't lose their money because of our robbery. Little by little, we could build a gang of wild-eyed hippies who would help us turn this country around.

It made perfect sense to a couple of drunk, drug-crazed lunatics. I thought our plan would be a way for me to win Misty's favor back, and possibly be reunited with her. I thought it would most certainly put me in a strong position to be the leader of the new SDS.

However, there was one small problem. We were down to our last dollars again, and we didn't have any guns. We needed guns to rob banks. And there was another problem—I didn't want to personally use a gun. From Mark's Vietnam War days, he had become proficient with all sorts of guns, rifles, and explosives. He had no problem with the idea of using weapons.

Mark asked around; one of his friends had a double-barreled, sawed-off 12-gauge shotgun, and he was willing to lend us the shotgun for a few days. Mark had told him we just wanted to do a little shooting practice. It was a good thing he gave us a handful of shotgun shells; I don't know whether we had enough money to buy any ammo.

John, our next-door neighbor who lived in a converted tool shed, had a .22-caliber tear gas igniter from his college days in the SDS. John said I could use his tear gas igniter, and that suited me just fine. I did not want a shotgun or handgun in my possession because I feared that I could actually use it if someone got in our way.

We had decided that before we tried to rob a bank, it would be best to rob a couple of easier targets, just to get the feel of things. Plus, Mark's friend who loaned us the shotgun informed us that it was a federal offense to have a sawed-off shotgun in your possession. The government

Story 11: Drugs & Guns

had made it a law back in the 1930s, when there had been a large number of bank robberies, and the robbers' weapon of choice was the sawed-off shotgun.

Well, that pretty well settled it for us, and confirmed our decision to pull off a couple of small heists before hitting a bank. Mark wanted a handgun before we moved up to the big leagues. After all, the sawed-off shotgun was fairly difficult to conceal, and it did carry that federal rap.

We barely had enough money to put a few dollars' worth of gas into Mark's 1950 Studebaker sedan. Not exactly a great getaway car. But it was time to put up or shut up. We drank the last of the cheap red wine and smoked a couple of joints.

Jumping into the Studebaker, we made our way to the Bettendorf Bridge over the Mississippi River, which would take us from the Illinois side of the river to the Iowa side. We had decided we would do all our robberies in Iowa—that would make it a lot easier for us to hide out in Illinois. When we crossed the river on that bridge, I was amazed, as I always was when I drove over that bridge, how wide the Mighty Mississippi really was.

We drove around for a little while, trying to decide what place looked most suitable for our crime. We settled on the Red Lion Hotel. It was just a couple of hundred yards from the entrance to the bridge that would take us safely back to Illinois.

We parked in the alley by the back door and left the engine running, because we were afraid it might not start—the car was temperamental. We wore navy blue stocking caps on our heads, and red bandanas pulled up over our noses. Only our beady little eyes were showing.

We walked down the hallway to the hotel's reception foyer. There were a few people in the area: one guy was reading a newspaper, and two other people were looking at postcards on a rack. Only one person was behind the check-in desk.

Nobody seemed to notice us. Had we entered the *Twilight Zone?* We looked at each other and shrugged our shoulders in dismay. We were prepared to say, "Everybody hit the ground," just like we'd seen done in the movies, but nobody looked at us. It was as if we were invisible.

So we turned our attention to the guy standing behind the desk fiddling with some paperwork. Mark pulled out the sawed-off shotgun from underneath his coat. He pointed it right in the clerk's face, and said, "Give me the money."

To our complete surprise, the clerk answered, "There isn't much money here. They have already turned in the receipts from the day shift. I work the night shift."

"Shut up!" Mark replied with an angry snarl. "Give me the damn money!"

With that command, the clerk rolled his eyes and shook his head in disbelief. He calmly opened the cash register and collected the cash from inside. Placing it on the counter in front of us, he said, "I told you there wasn't much."

Mark reached out with his left hand and grabbed the loot. The clerk actually said sorry when we turned to make our escape—as if apologizing for the lack of cash.

We headed down the hallway toward the door to the alley where the idling Studebaker waited for us. I had the .22 tear gas igniter, which wasn't much bigger than a small flashlight. Since nobody except the clerk seemed to notice us in the lobby, I saw no good reason to shoot the thing off in the hallway. I turned around one more time to see if anybody was following us. No one was in sight.

We jumped in the car, and Mark pushed down hard on the gas pedal to get us the hell out of there. I started unscrewing the head of the loaded tear gas cartridge, and to my utter shock, the damn thing ignited. The car instantly filled with tear gas.

Mark and I began to choke, cry, and cough. We couldn't see anything for about thirty seconds, and then Mark panicked. He put the pedal to the metal of that old Studebaker, and we burned rubber on the river road, swerving back and forth all the way down the road. We drove

Story 11: Drugs & Guns

right past the on-ramp to the bridge, tear gas smoke pouring out the windows.

Mark kept yelling, "Damn it, I can't see!"

I yelled back, "*Where in the hell are you going?*"

"I don't know! I'm just trying to get us out of here."

We drove down the river road for a few minutes, with the front windows rolled down. We cried and cried and cried! Finally, the gas cleared out enough, and Mark turned the car around to head back toward the bridge. We slowly turned onto the on-ramp of the Bettendorf Bridge, heading for Illinois, but we had barely gotten a couple of hundred yards on the bridge when Mark looked into the rearview mirror and said, "Oh, my god."

I was afraid to look behind, for fear that it would be bad—really bad. But with a jerk of my head, I turned around to see what he was seeing. It was an Iowa state trooper. His dark blue car had moved in behind us, and he was driving very slowly. But that didn't last long.

In a moment, red lights were flashing and sirens were blaring. A number of other Iowa state troopers had joined the chase. Mark increased his speed—until he realized that Illinois state troopers had set up a roadblock on the Illinois side of the Mississippi River. They were just a few hundred yards ahead of us.

Story 12:
Behind Bars

*An accident has never been blamed on
preparation or excellence.*
—Uncle Bear

The Illinois troopers had the bridge completely blocked off. They were standing outside their units with shotguns and handguns aimed right at us. Mark slammed on the brakes, and the car squealed to a halt.

The Iowa troopers behind us hit their brakes. In a show of impressive handling of their cars, as if they practiced this kind of stuff all the time, the two lead trooper units slid at a forty-five-degree angle to the left, then stopped.

One of the troopers demanded over a loudspeaker, "Get out of the car with your hands on your head."

Mark immediately jumped out with his hands on his head, but I just sat there, dazed and bewildered. I was considering jumping off the bridge into the Mississippi River, when I heard Mark yelling, "Marty! You crazy bastard! Get out of the car. They are going to shoot you!"

With Mark's desperate call to me, I snapped back to the reality of the moment. I slowly got out of the car and put my hands on my head. The troopers rushed in and forced each of us, face first, onto the hood of the car, while pulling our arms behind us; then they slapped on the handcuffs. The ride we took to the county jail is still a blur in my memory.

Story 12: Behind Bars

We had been on an alcohol and drug diet for days, weeks, maybe longer. It took a couple of days behind bars to fully realize that I was locked up in a jail somewhere in the Midwest, on the Mississippi River. I could not see the river, but I could smell its dank, muddy waters.

We were in the county jail in Davenport, Iowa, and would spend a month there before our arraignment. Every Friday night, a jailer would come and get me from the main lockup area of the men's quarters. The first Friday night, I was moved to an empty cell, with only a long bench in the middle of the room and a disgusting-looking one-piece metal toilet at the far end. I didn't understand why I was in this cell by myself.

The reason became evident as the night wore on. At around ten o'clock, a jailer unlocked and opened the barred-gate door of my empty cell, and ushered two very drunk fellows in to join me. I was more confused than ever as to why I was in this cell. About a half an hour later, the same jailer ushered in another drunk, and later two more drunks. It was starting to get crowded, and one of the drunks was throwing up all over the wall and floor in an attempt to hit the toilet.

It finally occurred to me that I was in the Friday night drunk tank. But I wondered why. At around midnight, it became obvious what the county jail guards were up to. It was 1970, in Iowa. I had grown my hair past my shoulders and sported a full beard. These drunks were, for the most part, farm-boy rednecks. The guards were hoping the drunks would beat the hell out of me, or worse. I spent four Friday nights in the drunk-tank, without once being beaten by any redneck. I think my guardian angel might have been with me.

Finally, after more than a month, it was time to go before the judge for my arraignment. "Young man, do you understand why you are standing before me today?" he asked.

"Yes, sir. But actually, I'm not exactly sure why I'm here."

"Well, young man, let me refresh your memory. You are being charged with conspiracy to overthrow the government of the United States."

To my utter shock and amazement, I laughed out loud, and said, *"What! You've got to be kidding me?"*

"Young man, may I remind you that this charge is very serious, and is not a laughing matter."

"No, Your Honor, it isn't in the least bit funny in any way, shape, or form, because the charge against me is erroneous and not true. I committed a very stupid crime of armed robbery, but I did not do anything to overthrow the government of the United States."

"May I remind you, young man, this is not a hearing, but only an arraignment procedure. Your attorney will have time to defend you at the actual hearing. However, at this present time, you are being charged with conspiracy to overthrow the government of the United States, which carries a thirty-year sentence in the state of Iowa."

I was guilty by association. I had always heard that birds of a feather flock together, but I didn't know the flock would all be charged with the same crime that another flock of birds had committed. I had friends in the SDS—Students for a Democratic Society—on campus in Chicago, New York, and Iowa City. I did hang out with a few yippies from the radical Youth International Party, and had met a couple of people who said they were members of the Weather Underground from Chicago. However, I never did meet or know anyone who was actually planning on overthrowing the United States government.

We had a variety of anti-Vietnam literature, a few antiestablishment psychedelic posters on the wall, and some SDS newspaper articles and pamphlets. Plus, I had a copy of Jerry Reuben's book, *DO IT!* Which was a very antiestablishment, crazy book. I thought we desperately needed change in the country, but not a violent revolution.

A growing number of people, both young and old, were showing signs of mental and emotional paranoia in those days. I first noticed people getting a little crazy because of the fiasco at the Democratic National Convention in Chicago, and the arrest and subsequent trial of the Chicago Seven.

Story 12: Behind Bars

The political and social unrest was at a boiling point because of the Ohio National Guard shooting students, wounding many, and actually killing four students. The students were nonviolent war protesters at Kent State University. Some of the students who were shot and killed were innocent bystanders; they weren't even involved in the anti-Vietnam War rally. It was getting crazy, and President Nixon was as paranoid as anyone in the country. It appeared that our president might just be a total control freak.

The shootings at Kent State ignited the largest-ever backlash of student protest marches and rallies at well over a hundred universities and colleges across the country, within days of the shooting. Thousands of students were now protesting at campuses in every state.

I was charged with conspiracy because in the eyes of the law, I was a genuine threat, and guilty by association. Our heinous and unbelievably stupid crime was that we stole $210 from a hotel at gunpoint. I had never been arrested before. But now, because of a lifestyle of drugs, alcohol abuse, and hanging out with the wrong crowd, I had potentially ruined my life. I was filled with deep-seated fear and bitterness. I felt trapped, and I desperately wanted out. I had to escape from this nightmare.

After spending more than a month in the Davenport County jail, I knew I would not be showing up for my actual trial. I could not bear the thought of spending God only knows how many years rotting in a federal prison during a thirty-year sentence.

I had one of those superficial jailhouse religious experiences, as in the saying, "There are no atheists in a foxhole." I did a whole lot of repenting while in jail, and asking God for his help. But my heart didn't change. I was really only trying to get some fire insurance from God.

Before leaving the state of Iowa after getting out on bail, I called Misty from the airport. "*Hey, Misty, it's Marty.*"

"Why are you calling me, you idiot?"

"*I'm calling you because I'm at the airport, about to catch a plane to California.*"

"They might be tapping the phone."

"*Misty, I really don't think they could be tapping this pay phone.*"

"Marty, let me make this perfectly clear. You are dead to me. You are a dead dog. Do not ever try to contact me again, ever!" And that was that—She hung up the phone on me with a clunk.

I was confused, but I didn't blame her. I had now officially become a loser. I thought, *Well at least I can save the thousand dollars that I owe her. Never the less, she will probably change her mind when I become a very wealthy man.* I was completely neurotic and extremely delusional.

I caught the first plane back to my old stomping grounds in Southern California. I took a bus from LAX to Disneyland. By chance, I called Will at his parents' house, and he was there. I asked him if he would pick me up at the big D. He said he would be there in five minutes. After picking me up, we dropped by my folks' house to say hi and thank them for bailing me out of jail. We then headed on to Laguna Beach, where we smoked some pot and drank a six-pack of beer with Danny the Dealer, a friend of ours who lived in Laguna Canyon. We crashed at his place for the night.

I was desperate to get out of the country before my upcoming trial date. They had released me on bail to California from Iowa. I needed to secure some housing and start the legit job that was waiting for me. I needed to see John Griggs, my childhood friend and founder of the Brotherhood of Eternal Love.

Story 13:
Out on Bail

*I learned the hard way that when life becomes its darkest,
the stars in the sky will shine their brightest.*
—Uncle Bear

Thanks to my brother, Jonnie, I had a construction job, hanging drywall in Southern Cal. I did the construction work for a couple of months, until I had a few hundred dollars in my pocket.

I bought a 1955 Mercedes 220E for $500. It was one of the last years of the Mercedes sedan round body style. The car was cool, and did not fit the stereotype of the common hippie. I reconnected with some friends of mine who lived in Hacienda Heights on a five-acre avocado grove. At the center of the five acres were two old Spanish-style haciendas. I moved into one of the homes with a friend who had started a jewelry company and was doing very well financially.

In the other house lived another friend of mine, who had started a health food honey import company. He imported fifty-gallon drums of organic honey from Columbia and other South American countries. Some of the drums of honey had kilos of marijuana in them. I later discovered that he was smuggling in cocaine as well.

I was selling kilos of marijuana to some people I had met in New York and Washington, DC. The money was really starting to roll in, but

I was running out of time. My trial was coming up in less than a month, and I had no intention of showing up for it.

I drove my Mercedes to Laguna Beach to connect with some of my friends in the Brotherhood. Farmer John Griggs, the leader of the Brotherhood, had actually incorporated the Brotherhood of Eternal Love as a California nonprofit corporation. It was definitely not non-profit—the Brotherhood made and sold more LSD than anyone else in the world.

I had thought John wanted to meet with me in Laguna Beach at his head shop, the Mystic Arts. When I arrived, I was told by some of the other Brothers that John was too paranoid regarding the heat; the police had been pressing in on the Brotherhood activities, especially in Laguna. He had driven up to the mountains, to the Brotherhood's lakeside ranch in Idyllwild. He wanted me to meet him there.

When I arrived, John was sitting on an Indian blanket in front of his teepee overlooking the lake.

"*Hey, John. How are you, brother?*"

"I'm cool, little brother. How is Jonnie?"

"*Not all that well. He has never been the same since being drafted. All the anxiety and fear that went along with the Vietnam War has left him very nervous and stressed-out.*"

"I'm sorry to hear that. Jonnie was always so much fun to be with, all the way back to our elementary school days at Lincoln School."

My brother had been all about fun and water sports. He loved to surf, glide through the water on his jet ski, or sail with the breeze in his sailboat.

"Marty, I understand that you got yourself into a dump load of trouble in the Midwest."

"*Yeah, I'm afraid that would be a major understatement.*"

"Because you and your brother have always been like family to me, I want to help you get out of this mess you've gotten yourself into."

"*Thanks John, I don't know what to say. How do you think I can get out of this mess?*"

Story 13: Out on Bail

"I really do believe you were on the path of enlightenment. I'm totally cool with Jesus. As a matter of fact, the Brothers and I have been reading the Bible recently, and we are convinced that Israel is at the epicenter of the future for planet earth and its inhabitants."

"Wow! I was not expecting to hear that coming from you."

"Why not, little brother? I meant it when I said we were cool with Jesus. It seems to me that he was very focused on loving God, and loving all the people, all the time. The Brotherhood is 100 percent behind what he stood for and what he was trying to accomplish."

"What do you think he was trying to accomplish?"

"Peace! Everywhere he went he proclaimed peace, and that is exactly what we want—peace on earth and goodwill toward man."

"I get the feeling you are going somewhere with this."

"Yes, little brother, you have a keen perception for the obvious. The Brotherhood would like to front you ten thousand tabs of Orange Sunshine."

"That is a lot of LSD. What do you want me to do with it?"

"We want you to go to Israel and make contact with a Palestinian friend of ours."

"Do you want me to give him ten thousand tabs of Orange Sunshine?"

"No, that would not be wise or practical to just give him thousands of dollars' worth of our LSD. We do, however, want to sell it to him at a really low price. We are convinced that the only way to divert the end of the world, as we know it, is by turning on the Palestinians and the Israelis to LSD.

"The money is not the issue with us. As a matter of fact, we want you to keep all the proceeds from the sale of the Sunshine." *"Far-out! What do you think I should do after the sale of the LSD?"* "That, little brother, is exactly the right question to ask—and we will talk over the details after we eat some organic fruit that I picked this morning."

At the end of the day, I had in my possession over ten thousand tabs of Orange Sunshine LSD and a plan. Naïve as we were, the Brotherhood really did believe that LSD could help bring about a revolution of love around the world. We were genuine flower children. The seed of our dream was LSD, and the fertilizers for the dream were hashish and marijuana. The Brotherhood believed that only psychoactive psychedelic substances could bring about world peace and enlightenment.

The plan was for me to sell some of the LSD in Europe, and then move to the Middle East to sell the lion's share of the psychedelic Orange Sunshine. Farmer John Griggs was convinced that LSD could help bring peace in the Middle East. After selling the rest of my LSD in Israel for only one dollar per tab, I was to fly to India.

The Brotherhood had a medical doctor in Bombay who they had worked with on previous occasions. For the right amount of money, he would falsify my death. Falsifying my death would accomplish three steps of the plan. First, it would get the FBI off my tail. They would close my case for good once they learned that I was dead and buried.

That would allow the accomplishment of step two of the plan. Obviously, I would not be in the old wooden coffin. The corrupt doctor from Bombay would officially say on the documents that I had died of some horrible, very contagious disease. Similar documents would be glued to the outside of the coffin, encouraging US Customs officials to not open the coffin, for fear the disease might spread to them and others.

Which brings me to the beauty of step two. Since I would not be in the coffin, we would need to fill it with something that would equal my weight. So we thought it would be best to fill the coffin with 180 pounds of hashish. After my funeral, some of my hometown Brotherhood friends would go to the cemetery and dig up my coffin. The hashish would be sold by the pound. It would probably take less than two weeks to sell it all in Laguna and Newport Beach.

Then it would be time for step three. One of the well-trusted Brotherhood dealers would fly to Goa, India to meet me, with the money from the sale of the hashish. The money would be given to me. The friend who delivered the money would be my full partner in the hashish trade.

Story 13: Out on Bail

We would then have a sailboat custom built for us, and it would have one thousand pounds of hashish sealed in the keel. The Brotherhood had done this a few times before, with boat builders in Goa, and the Afghan hashish connection was thought to be secure.

When the sailboat was finished, we would fly in a seasoned, trusted crew to sail it across the Pacific Ocean to Maui, Hawaii. This method of sailing, with a competent, knowledgeable crew, had been used by the Brotherhood on previous sailings from India. I would be aboard the sailboat, with all new identification saying that I was a Canadian citizen. This would be the beginning of a new life for me. I was excited, and ready to make an undocumented and nonrefundable leap of faith into my new life.

After our meeting, Farmer John wanted to drive to Laguna Beach and have a celebration dinner at the White House restaurant with two other members of the Brotherhood. I was surprised when the two other members were Timothy Leary and his son. I had originally met Leary at a "Love In" at San Francisco's Golden Gate Park. The second time we chatted was at the University of New York at Buffalo and our last encounter was at a "Human Be-in" outside of Iowa City on a lush grassy hill overlooking a green valley of spring corn.

This was the last time I would ever see Timothy Leary or John Griggs.

Break on Through to the Other Side

Marty at celebration dinner in Laguna Beach

Story 14:
Maui Wowi

*Fear is faith in reverse
fear can be a claustrophobic
dark room with a dead-bolted exit.
Freedom is always on the other side of fear.
Thinking endlessly about it has never unlocked the door
Only transformative prayerful decisive action will set you free.*
—Uncle Bear

The Brotherhood of Eternal Love had considerable property holdings on the island of Maui. The infamous Maui Wowi was marijuana planted by the Brotherhood, using hybrid Mexican and Panamanian seeds. Mules were people who volunteered, or were paid, to carry suitcases with kilos of Maui Wowi back to the mainland during the sixties and early seventies.

On occasion, one of the sailboats built in Goa would arrive with a keel full of Afghan hashish. Only the best and most trusted mules would carry loads of hash back to the mainland, where it would be sold.

It was now time for me to initiate step one of the plan. I concealed the ten thousand plus tabs of Orange Sunshine LSD in my luggage and flew to New York, where I bought a one-way ticket to Amsterdam on KLM Dutch Airlines.

The all-night flight was seamless, and I did not sleep a wink. I was just too excited to leave the good ole USA. Upon arrival, I met with a couple of guys who had done several business deals with the Brotherhood during the past year. They helped me sell a couple of hundred tabs of Orange Sunshine LSD, which gave me some traveling money.

I made my way to the mountains of Switzerland. I had heard of the University of the New World in Switzerland. An extension campus from New York had recently commenced their first classes there. The college was in the Alps, high above the Rhone Valley, in a small Swiss village called Haute-Nendaz. I rented a chalet in Haute-Nendaz on a month-to-month basis. I could easily blend in with all the other Americans attending this new extension campus.

Unfortunately, from what I was told, the University of the New World extension of some New York college was a scam. The only thing the would-be students had to show for their unfortunate college investment was the commercial and residential buildings in Haute-Nendaz that had been rented by the university in the early stages of the scam.

Many of the students just stayed in the rented housing for the winter. I sold them just enough LSD and hashish to keep me in spending money, yet somewhat under the radar. This gave me the time I needed to plan my move to Israel. A good number of Jews from New York City had journeyed to Switzerland to be part of this new international university.

We had long talks about Israel. I was surprised at how many of them had already been there. A few had actually worked as volunteers on kibbutzim. Volunteer worker on a kibbutz sounded like a perfect way for me to blend in, and learn as much as I could about the Israelis and Palestinians.

I was ready to fly off to Israel, but I needed to take care of one more detail in Frankfurt, Germany, before I left Europe for the kibbutz life in Israel. A mule carrier was flying in from California with more Orange Sunshine LSD for me to smuggle into Israel.

Plus, I wanted to sell my VW bus in Germany, where I had bought it. I had paid $300 for the bus from an American GI stationed near Frankfurt, who was being discharged in thirty days. It was pretty common

Story 14: Maui Wowi

knowledge that you could get a really good deal from GIs who were "short," meaning their time in the military was coming to a close.

After the sale of my bus, I would take a train back to Switzerland, and fly from there to Israel. Because Switzerland had a more peaceful international reputation than any other country in Europe, I felt it was my best chance at freely passing through customs in Israel.

I knew the date and time of my mule's arrival at the Frankfurt airport. He was an acquaintance of mine from Anaheim, called Slim Jim for obvious reasons; he was as skinny as a rail. Jim desperately wanted to be accepted into the Brotherhood. He was to meet me at Pot Luck Park, the name local German hippies called a park in Frankfurt where a lot of dealing was done. Jim was to meet me at the park at noon the day after his arrival.

I went to the park that day in the late morning and waited for the mule. I was sitting on the far side of the park's man-made lake, feeding some ducks. I looked up, and noticed my mule was in the park and dealing out in the open, as if it was legal or something. I thought, *This idiot thinks he is in Disneyland.*

I knew he would get busted if he kept that up for much longer. So I strolled over to the other side of the lake to clue him in on the local legal scene. I greeted him, then asked, "*What in the hell are you doing, dealing so openly?*"

He reacted arrogantly "Hey Man, I can deal right under the pigs' noses, and they won't even know it."

I told him that I had known it from all the way across the lake, and convinced him to leave the park immediately. We headed for his VW bus, which he had purchased prior to his arrival.

Unbeknown to me, he had a friend in Frankfurt who had already set him up with a VW bus waiting for him at the airport. He said my cut of the LSD was at his German friend's pad. I knew the German hippie he was referring to.

I was visibly upset with Jim for leaving my stash at a German hippie's pad. He explained, "Marty, I'm sorry man. I know I should not have left your LSD at the German's place, but I didn't want to come out in public with it."

"*It was my understanding that you were supposed to put it in a locker at the Frankfurt train station.*"

"Well that's just it; I didn't come into town by train. I drove into Frankfurt in my VW bus."

"*I am fully aware that you drove the VW, but that was not the original plan.*"

"You are right man, I should have followed the plan. I'm really sorry—please let me make it up to you."

"*How do you think you can make it up to me?*"

"In the VW bus, I have a pound of hashish, and I would like to give you an ounce of prime black Afghan hash."

Stupidly, I agreed to go to his van to get my gift.

When he turned the key in the door of the van to unlock it, there was a roar of rustling commotion coming at us from all directions. The German police had already staked out the van, and were just waiting for the owner to return.

Without a moment's notice, I was slammed against the side window of the van. Then I felt the cold steel of the barrel of a German police gun pressed against my temple. I thought, *Damn, if he is trigger-happy, I am a dead man.*

I could not believe how many German police there were. It was as if they were coming out of the bushes and falling from the trees.

The next thing I knew, a pair of handcuffs were slammed onto my hands, which were being held behind my back. The police kept yelling at us in German, and I could not understand what they were saying. But I did interpret enough to know one thing—I was in a huge predicament, with no visible route of escape.

Story 15:
Get Out of Dodgendorf

*When fear casts its shadow of darkness upon you,
look for the light,
and be satisfied to know that without darkness,
there would be no light.*
—Uncle Bear

I could not believe what was happening to me. I was being rushed off to the local German police station because of the idiot mule's dealing out in the open at a public park. He should have been laying low until he had delivered the locker key to me.

Stupid me! I thought. *Why in the world did I go to his van?* Confused, my thoughts rambled. *They are taking me to the police station, and they will run a background check on me, and they are going to hit the jackpot when they find out the FBI is looking for me. Stupid is as stupid does.*

I was on the FBI's most wanted list because of the nature of my crime, and mainly because I had jumped bail and left the country. I was already facing a thirty-year sentence, and now they could add another ten years for jumping bail. I was so screwed.

When they got me to the police station, everything went just as I thought it would. There was a lot of yelling in German, then an interpreter would yell at me in English. They took my passport, and were running a background check on me.

I sat there in a half-dazed stupor, waiting for the door to fly open, revealing a German detective standing in the door-way, beaming with an ear-to-ear smile. But it never happened.

They interrogated me for something like two hours. My main story was "*The van is not mine. I just met this American, and he was going to give me some hashish.*"

I knew the VW bus had already been searched with a fine-tooth comb. They would have found the hashish and whatever amount of Orange Sunshine LSD he possessed.

They did discover that I had a German VW van of my own. *Had the mule told them?* He was probably trying to help me out. I had never registered it in my name. It was registered to an American girl I had met at the Frankfurt youth hostel. She was a Southern belle for sure—and she did have a brief romantic thing for me, and I for her. However, I knew she was not the girl of my dreams.

They questioned me at length about my van. All I would tell them is that I had only part ownership in it, and that the other person had the van. I told them over and over that I didn't know where in Germany she was currently driving it. I actually knew she had safely flown back to the States two weeks prior.

I spent the night in jail. Of course, I did very little sleeping that night, wondering what would happen in the morning. It was a very long night. I actually had the nerve to ask God for help. It was one of those *God save my skin, but don't change my heart* kind of prayers.

Eventually, morning did come, and with it only a cup of crappy, lukewarm coffee and two stale cookies. I sat in the cell for a couple more hours, wondering if they would ever feed me something. Fear of the inevitable wore on the walls of my empty stomach. I felt hopeless and trapped, awaiting my execution.

Finally, the door to my cell flew open. A German policeman greeted me with a scowl, and said, "You go now," as he pointed his finger toward the hallway to his right.

Story 15: Get Out of Dodgendorf

I followed his lead, and the next thing I knew, I was standing in the reception area of the station, where the not-so-friendly detective handed me my passport and said, "Please, you will now leave Germany."

I thought, *Oh, hell yes! I am out of here.*

I walked all the way back to where I had parked my van. I purposely zig-zagged up and down streets, alleyways, over fences, and around the block a few times. I must have walked a few miles just to make sure I was not being followed.

When I reached my van, I took a deep breath and felt for my hidden key under the front bumper. I had by instinct hidden it there before I took my walk in the park the day before. I drove off, holding my breath. There weren't any red lights flashing or sirens blaring. Nevertheless, I broke out in a cold sweat. My mind was racing with all kinds of paranoid thoughts. One thought kept recurring: *I've got to get out of this country.*

I went to the German hippie's place to pick up my LSD. He was pleasant, and getting my package from him happened without incident. He asked, "Where is Slim Jim?"

I mischievously remarked, "*He said he wanted to spend some time with new friends he had met.*"

The acreage nearby was an open, hilly area just outside Frankfurt. I had actually walked this landscape before, after I had gotten loaded at the German hippie's pad. I remembered a very old, and extremely large, oak tree that was near the top of one of the hills. I had sat under it to cool off in its massive shaded canopy. I decided that was where I would bury my stash of LSD, and I did just that. I desperately needed a vacation from the police and the smuggling world.

I was a nervous reck from my twenty-four hour ordeal with the German police. I drove from Frankfurt straight to Munich, sold my van in only an hour in front of the train station youth hostel, for three hundred dollars. I checked into the youth hostel—it was a bit stressful giving the manager my passport for the night. However, I really didn't have any other viable options in front of me.

I was beginning to relax a little from all the insane stress I had been through the previous two days. A late evening meal at a local Italian restaurant was greatly enjoyed. I ordered an extra-large pizza and a huge pitcher of beer. I shared my pizza and the beer with some young people in the restaurant. It was good fun and a needed mental break from my stressful universe.

It was time to go to the youth hostel, take a shower, and get plenty of sleep before the long trip that awaited me the next day. After the warm, wonderful shower, I organized my belongings in my duffel bag, and chose the lower level of a bunk bed in the farthest corner from the entry to the massive dorm bunkroom.

The lights went out at 10:00 p.m. sharp, as was the custom of every youth hostel in Germany. I had already rolled into the bunk in the corner when the lights went off. I melted into the bed—my tight muscles began to relax—sleep found me quickly.

In a flash of white light, the bright ceiling bulbs illuminated the dorm bunkroom. I squinted my eyes to see who was standing at the entry doorway of the bunkroom. It was the manager and a policeman. Together, they scanned the room, looking for someone. Suddenly, the manager pointed in my direction.

The manager and the policeman began to quickly march across the room, headed for me. When they got to my bunk, the policeman reached out with his huge open hands. The muscles of his long arms bulged as he extended them toward me. With a groan, I anticipated what would happen in the next second. But he passed me by, and reached under my bunk to grab a young boy. The German teenager cried out in dreadful pleas as they dragged him from the room.

The door slammed shut, and the lights went off. I lay there awake in the darkness. My heart raced from the surge of adrenaline into my bloodstream. With much anxiety, I tried to relax and go back to sleep, but sleep did not find me for at least two more hours.

Story 16:
Escape to Ios

*You never know you have been asleep,
until you experience waking up.*
—Uncle Bear

The morning sunlight beamed across the bunkroom and softly awakened me. I took a train ride to the Munich International Airport, and bought a one-way ticket to Athens, Greece. At the airport, I went to the men's restroom. As I sat minding my natural business, I could not help but notice how many things had been written on the walls of the stall. They were written in various languages, but one that was written in English caught my attention. I read it and pondered the meaning of the admonition.

I will instruct you and teach you in the way you should go. I will guide you with my eye upon you. Psalm 32

The jetliner lifted off the runway, leaving Munich behind us. It felt as though a thousand pounds fell from my shoulders. My breathing slowed down, and for the first time in forty-eight hours, I could take deep breaths that temporarily filled my soul with a shallow tranquility.

I fell asleep within minutes of takeoff. I was awakened an hour later by a stewardess. She asked me if I wanted anything. I opened my eyes and looked up. I liked what I saw in the warm smile of the young lady leaning toward me. She asked me again, "May I get you anything?"

I smiled, and sheepishly asked, *"Are you on the menu?"*

She blushed and said, "No, I'm sorry. Would you like something to drink?"

"*Yes, I would love an ice-cold beer.*"

She looked puzzled, "I'm sorry, you would like ice in your beer?"

"*No, I only meant that I wanted a cold beer.*"

"Is German beer good for you?"

"*Yes, a cold German beer would be wonderful.*"

The lunch they served on the flight later was pitiful. So I had another beer and a bag of nuts.

We arrived at the Athens International Airport on time. Customs was a breeze, and I took a public bus to the Port of Piraeus. I was stoked and surprised to learn that a boat was leaving within the hour for five Greek islands. Ios was one of the islands the boat would visit on its round trip, and Ios was where I wanted to go.

I quickly purchased a round-trip ticket to the small Greek island. I was informed that these particular islands were visited only once a week. Having keen perception of the obvious, I then knew I would be staying for at least a week on Ios.

An international mix of well-traveled hippies in Switzerland had told me if I ever wanted to get away from it all, I should check out the Greek Island of Ios. I definitely wanted to get away from it all.

The boat voyage to Ios was very relaxing. I made immediate friends with some old, crusty-looking Greek fishermen. They introduced me to the favorite liquor of Greece, ouzo. It was funny stuff—a clear liquid until mixed with water. Then it turned kind of a milky-white color, and tasted like black licorice.

When we arrived at the port of Ios, I discovered there wasn't a port. All I saw was an old, dilapidated wooden dock. The boat pulled up as close as it could without touching, for fear the old dock would collapse.

What looked to be a long, weather-beaten wooden plank was lowered from the side of the boat to the rickety, dry-rotted dock. The plank was no more than two inches thick by eighteen inches wide—and the swells of the Aegean Sea were at least five to six feet.

Story 16: Escape to Ios

Two of the salt weathered old fishermen walked down the plank like it was a three-foot-wide gangway. I grabbed my duffel bag, and took my turn at walking the plank. As I made my way down it, the swell momentarily turned into an eight-foot plunge.

I panicked and made a dash for the dock. I could see that within a split second, the boat would be lower than the dock, so I lunged forward, leaping with my right leg first. I felt my right foot hit the edge of the dock with a thump—but at the same time, I could feel my left leg going down lower than I thought possible.

The crotch of my well-worn Levi's completely ripped out. Both of the fishermen who had gone down the plank before me reached out, grabbed me by the shoulders, and pulled me to safety. I stood there for a moment in shock, thoroughly embarrassed. I wasn't wearing any underwear.

From the roar of their laughter, the locals on the shore thought this was one of the funniest things they had ever seen. What can you do when everyone is laughing at you?

I proceeded to take my bows and thank the crowd for their cheerful acceptance of my arrival.

Story 17:
The Island Is Ours

*The true success of a vessel at sea is weighed against
the hope of its returning safely home.*
—Uncle Bear

In the port of Ios was a makeshift little bar of sorts, where I asked a couple of really crusty, sunbaked hippies where the action was. They told me I would find it on the other side of the island.

"*The other side of the island!*" I replied.

"Yeah, man, you just follow that dirt road over there, up the hill and keep on going, and you will end up on the other side of the island."

"*How long of a walk is it?*"

"It's only an hour or so to the top of the hill. Once you get to the top, you will be in the only little village on Ios. There you will want to get a beer and sit down for a few minutes. You will see some other freaks hanging out, and you might want to ask them where Yawny's is."

"*Why is it called Yawny's?*"

"Well, man, his real name is Johnny, but the locals pronounce it Yawny. It is where all the freaks eat, just about every night."

"*Why do all the hippies eat there?*"

"Simple, man. It's a buck a plate load."

"*What does he serve?*"

Story 17: The Island Is Ours

"We don't know, and trust me, you don't want to find out. It is always some kind of stew or something. The grub fills your tummy, and you can buy a bottle of cheep Greek wine for another dollar. It doesn't get any better on Ios. Of course, usually somebody is passing around a joint or a pipe of hash. It's cool, you'll see."

After my brief stop at the top of the hill and a quick beer at Yawny's, I was on my way. The walk down the hill to the other side of the island was really pleasant. There it was, a sight to behold—something like two hundred hippies, spread out across the white sands of an absolutely breathtaking bay with turquoise blue waters.

There were tents, makeshift lean-tos, and sleeping bags everywhere. It was truly an international mix of hippies from Europe, Canada and the United States. There was no police, or anyone telling you what you could or couldn't do. The island of Ios was ours.

After a couple of days of sunshine and salt water, I discovered that it cost a dollar to get hosed off by a local Greek opportunist, who owned the deepest well on the island. It was a buck well spent, and the locals loved the US dollar. I don't know what the European hippies used to pay for all the one-dollar specials on Ios.

After two weeks of birthday suit swimming and fun in the sun, I began to think about my LSD stash back in Germany. I knew I could not hang out on my Greek fantasy island forever. I needed to get back on track, in the direction of the big picture and the bigger plan.

I was also starting to get numb and dumb from all the partying. It seemed like one endless party, from sunup to sundown. It was as if I was trying to drown my guilt and fear by drinking, smoking pot and eating my way into stupor-land.

I said good-bye to all my new hippie friends, and walked over to the other side of Ios to catch the only boat back to Athens that week. Within seventy-two hours, I was back in Frankfurt, Germany.

Break on Through to the Other Side

Marty and a friend walking in forest outside Frankfurt

Story 18:
Bombs Away

*Becoming detached from your ego
could mean you have arrived at psychosis,
or maybe you are now ready to discover your true self.*
—Uncle Bear

The flight back to Frankfurt had gone very smoothly. I went to the main youth hostel by the Rhine River, in downtown Frankfurt. I saw a German hippie I knew, and he offered to give me a ride in his car. He drove me to the hills just outside Frankfurt, where I had buried my stash. I told him that I just needed a little space and time alone in nature. He asked me if I wanted him to wait for me, so that I would have a ride back to the hostel. I told him I would catch a bus back into downtown Frankfurt. He was cool with that and said he would see me later tonight at the little river park in front of the hostel.

I walked around for a while, so I'd look like the average casual hiker. When I felt it was safe, I walked up to the enormous old oak tree on the hillside, where I had buried my LSD. I had to rehearse in my memory what I had done before. I could visualize the experience in my mind's eye.

From the trunk of the tree, I needed to head in the direction of the big black rock. I counted off the twenty-two paces, and stood above the very spot where I thought I had buried my stash. I dug down into the wet, cold ground with my bare hands. I panicked a little when it was not where I thought it should be. I paused, thought about it for a few minutes, and looked around to see if anyone was watching me.

Vigorously, I returned to my digging. I was like a dog searching for a bone it had previously hidden. *Where the hell is it?* I began to wonder if someone had seen me bury it. Maybe someone had ripped me off. I knew that wasn't uncommon in this illegal business.

I grabbed a nearby stick and widened the path of my frantic digging, not willing to accept defeat. Finally, my nearly frozen fingers could feel something like, yes, the plastic bag. I pulled it from the ground, and quickly brushed it off.

I tucked it into my backpack and quickly left the area. Strangely, it didn't feel like I was carrying thousands of dollars' worth of LSD. I reminded myself that it was, indeed, worth many thousands of dollars. The walk back to the bus stop was longer than I had remembered, but I enjoyed every step along the way. I felt like my life was back on track, to fund my great escape.

I booked a flight from Frankfurt, Germany to Tel Aviv, Israel for the day after the next. I thought it would be safe to crash at the pad of a couple German hippie friends, but I didn't tell a living soul what I was carrying to Israel. I stayed two nights with my German friends. They did wonder why I was in such a rush to leave Germany and head to Israel.

The morning of my flight, I began to load the LSD into my body belt, as I had done previously. But I began to feel very uncomfortable about placing it in the usual compartments of the body belt. There was a voice in my head saying, "Don't put it there."

I heeded the warning of the mysterious voice. I placed before me each of the little individual bags of the tabs of Orange Sunshine. Each bag wasn't much bigger than a small walnut. I rolled as many as I could into the neck of a thick, woven turtleneck sweater. Others went into pairs of socks, the pockets of my only other two pairs of pants, and my sleeping bag. Jackpot! There was a rip in one corner of my well-worn sleeping bag. I stuffed the remainder of the LSD in the sleeping bag.

Story 18: Bombs Away

After I had hidden away all my stash, it was time to get going to the airport. My German hippie friends were mentally a little on the dark side of the moon, but I didn't know anyone else I could trust at the time to stay with. The next morning, they gave me a ride in their VW bus to the Frankfurt International Airport.

While I was standing in line for check-in, I happened to notice three German police vans pulling up to the curb at the Lufthansa Airlines terminal. They were the Frankfurt Germany SWAT team, a highly trained police squad that was highly feared by all drug dealers in Germany.

They were obviously here for some kind of serious ordeal. They were in full SWAT regalia, with helmets, bulletproof vests, machine guns, and two German Shepherd K-9s. There must have been at least a dozen men on the SWAT team.

They moved quickly into the large entry hall of the Lufthansa check-in lines, fanned out, and moved forward with disciplined, cautious steps. People moved away from them as they tightened the circle of their approach.

Suddenly, I was aware that they seemed to be closing in on me. I tried to step aside, but one of the SWAT policemen yelled, "Nein!" and pointed his machine gun at me. Before I could say, "*What the hell?*" I was surrounded by the German police SWAT team.

I stood still with my hands raised high in the air. I was even more dumbfounded when four other SWAT team members brought in what appeared to be large panels and a folding table. Within a few minutes, they had set up four walls of a makeshift enclosure.

Four SWAT team members stood guard, with machine guns aimed directly at me. The other SWAT guys were carefully moving the bystanders away from me in every direction. This was all way too weird.

I was invited to join two of the SWAT team inside the enclosure. In broken English, one said, "You will please take clothes off."

I said, "*What?*"

His voice got louder, and a bit angry, "Off with clothes!"

I began to take my clothes off, right in the middle of the huge Lufthansa Airlines terminal. No one could see me inside the partitions except the two policemen, but I could feel the stares of hundreds of eyes looking in my direction. I thought, *Why in the hell are they doing this?* The other guy, who wasn't yelling at me, began to dump all my belongings onto the table. I thought for a moment, *Wow, if I had worn my body belt, I would be busted for sure.*

I tried to watch without obvious nervousness as they picked up each item of clothing, gave it a little feel, and then placed it to the other side of the table. *There goes my sweater—he didn't feel the neck. There goes a pair of socks—he didn't feel the tabs of LSD.* He picked up my sleeping bag, looked at me, and said, "Dirty, this bag dirty."

I forced a smile, and agreed with him wholeheartedly "*Yes, dirty. Very old and very dirty.*"

In disgust, he mumbled, "Hippies." And then he said the all-time ass kicker, "You must now leave Germany!"

"Yes, sir. I'm leaving right now. Today I fly to Israel."

And then it hit me. They weren't looking for drugs. They were looking for some kind of bomb or explosive. I was flying to Israel! I was flying from Germany on EL AL, the Israeli airline.

I think my idiot German friends thought they would pull a little practical joke on me by calling in a bomb threat at the airport, and giving them my description. Some German hippies had a very dark, distorted sense of humor.

They had no idea I was holding a few thousand tabs of Orange Sunshine LSD. I had told no one that I had such a stash, and I definitely hadn't told anyone that I was wanted by the FBI.

Story 19:
Kibbutz Gonen

*Faith is the father of experience,
as hope is the mother of dreams.*
—Uncle Bear

I can't remember much of what happened the next hour or so after the German SWAT team came to send me off to Israel. I guess I was in some form of stress shock, or some other kind of mental illness. It's one of those experiences you can never be prepared for, or would want to be prepared for.

I did notice that everyone with me on the plane to Israel seemed to treat me with a strange sort of respect—or was it caution? A couple of young Israeli soldiers on board caught my eye and smiled broadly, both of them giving me the international approval sign of thumbs up.

The flight to Israel seemed like a magic carpet ride. In a strange way, I felt like I was flying home for the very first time. I drank two of the last German beers I would have for many months.

Passing through customs at the Tel Aviv airport was a little nerve-racking. I had heard that they rarely searched people flying into Israel, but not this day! They were searching dear little old men and little old ladies. I mean they were seriously going through everyone's luggage.

I actually stood by the luggage conveyor belt and watched my duffel bag go by three times. I considered leaving without picking up my bag with all the LSD in it. Each time it passed by me, I thought about how much it was worth. Then I would think about how many years I would be in prison for conspiracy to overthrow the United States government, international smuggling, and being a fugitive at large. I was smack dab in the middle of a radical dilemma, and in heart-pounding indecision.

Finally, on the fourth trip around the conveyor belt, I thought, *Oh, what the hell!* I grabbed my duffel bag, and headed straight for the shortest customs line. I tried to slow everything down. I could feel the adrenaline rushing into my head from the overwhelming fear I was experiencing. I kept telling myself, *I'm not going to get caught. I'm not going to get caught.* Before I joined the line of travelers going through customs, I shifted gears with these final thoughts, *Walk slowly Marty and take smooth deep breaths.*

The customs officer searched the crap out of the luggage of the well-dressed middle-aged couple in front of me. I thought, *Oh, I am so screwed.* He finally passed them through. Then he looked at me with dark brown, piercing eyes. He had the thickest black hairy eyebrows I had ever seen. He motioned with his hand, and said, "You're next."

I forced a stupid smile, and nervously said, "*How are you today? Catch anybody yet?*"

He looked directly into my eyes and said, "No, not yet, but I will." I was about to pee my pants until I heard him say, "Have a nice day, and enjoy your stay in Israel."

I smiled from ear to ear, "*And you, too. Have a nice day!*" I could have kissed him right then and there.

I caught a cab just outside the terminal. I asked the driver, "*Do you know what is going on in customs today?*"

"Yes, I think they are looking for diamonds, gold, and other gemstones." I thought, *Can anything else weird happen today?* But I had a strange feeling that more weirdness was coming my way.

The same multinational group of hippies who had told me about the island of Ios had told me about a kibbutz in the very north of Israel. They assured me that Kibbutz Gonen was the place to be a volunteer

Story 19: Kibbutz Gonen

worker. Food was in abundance, they said, and it was by far the most beautiful area in Israel.

I had the taxi driver take me to the public bus station. I located the bus that was going to the northern Galilee town of Kiriot Shamoni. Before reaching the town, I was told to tell the bus driver to let me out at the crossroad that would lead to Kibbutz Gonen.

I got in line—or a queue, as the British would say—except there was a problem. These people didn't have a clue what a queue was. Everyone just pushed and shoved around the bus door entrance. A Palestinian woman started up the steps in front of me, to board the bus. A Palestinian man grabbed her by the hair, and threw her backward to the ground. He angrily yelled some Arabic words at her, and then he boarded the bus. I tried to help her up, but she declined my assistance, and said in broken English, "Only make worse, you make worse." Nobody else even seemed to notice what had just happened, and it was obvious they couldn't care less.

I boarded the bus, reminding myself that I was only a visitor in this country. The Israeli bus driver was really a trip. He made a couple of people get up from the front seat across from him so I could sit next to him, across the aisle. He was kind of a hippie wannabe. As soon as we left the bus station, he raised his hand, waving an eight-track audiotape in the air.

He smiled and said, "This cool, you will like." Then he slammed it into the eight-track player mounted on the dash. From the two speakers mounted on either side of the dashboard blared the voice of Cat Stevens, singing "Miles from Nowhere." He was playing Cat Stevens's album *Tea for the Tillerman.*

I must admit I was impressed by his choice of music. After Cat Stevens, he played *Sgt. Pepper's Lonely Hearts Club Band* from his Beatles collection. To say the least, it was a trippy ride through the desert and hills of Israel. We passed the Sea of Galilee, and were headed north through the Golan Heights. The sun was beginning to set when the bus driver pointed ahead with his finger and said, "Mount Hermon, you see, Mount Hermon."

I agreed with him and said, "*Oh yeah. I see it.*" I didn't have a clue what he was pointing at.

The sun had already set by the time we reached northern Galilee. I was beginning to worry a little about where in the world I was going in the dark of night. It didn't help my nerves any when I noticed there were a lot more Palestinians on the bus than Israelis.

Without any notice, the bus came to an unexpected breakneck stop, in what appeared to be in the middle of nowhere. The bus door swung open. A warm desert breeze blew dust and sand into my face. The driver pointed with his hand and said, "Gonen, Kibbutz Gonen that way."

Story 20:
Jerusalem, Jerusalem

*One of the greatest challenges in life is to simply see reality
clearly for what it is, not for what you think you see,
or what you wish you could see.
It is how you see that makes all the difference in the world.*
—Uncle Bear

I got off the bus at the location the bus driver claimed was the road to Kibbutz Gonen. The bus pulled away in a cloud of diesel exhaust and dust. There was absolutely no light in the middle of the desert, and my eyes had not yet adjusted to the darkness. It was then I realized there was no moon in the sky. I could vaguely make out the road in front of me.

Slowly, very slowly, I took baby steps in the direction I hoped would lead me to the Kibbutz. Weird things can run through your mind in the black of night in the middle of nowhere, with the desert wind making strange sounds. All kinds of terrifying thoughts started to run through my head about what might happen to me on this desolate road.

Just when I was about to give up and sit down on the side of the road, hoping to just make it through the night, I saw a glimmer of light ahead of me, in what appeared to be a hill. Within a few minutes, I could see the light in all its glory. The full moon was rising over the hills of the Golan Heights. It was spectacular, and it was rising directly in front of me. I could see the road, and it was lined with flourishing, tall poplar trees on either side of the road. The strange sounds I had heard in the dark of night had been none other than the soft desert breeze blowing through the leaves of the towering poplars.

I spontaneously gave thanks to God, and shortly thereafter I began to laugh like a crazy person, thinking, *Oh yeah, Marty. God Almighty did this just for you. You have completely forgotten God, and now you think He has done this just for you? You are sick, Martin Berry, you are definitely delusional.*

To my complete, utter shock, I felt the presence of the voice. The same voice that had spoken into my thoughts in my bedroom back home when I asked, *Is Jesus the truth?*

Once again, I heard the voice in my thoughts, saying, "I am with you."

I thought, *Is it possible that God is with me, even though I have turned my back on Him? Well, I guess it is possible. After all, if He is God, He can do whatever He wants to do.*

I pondered these things for the remainder of my four-mile walk to the Kibbutz.

The lights of Gonen, with the full moon rising above it, was such a pleasant sight to behold as I got closer to the end of a very long, stressful day. Palm trees were waving in the gentle breeze, welcoming me. Other mature trees, bushes, and bunches of pampas grass filled in the landscape, with little homes well-placed throughout the Kibbutz.

I came upon two people walking hand in hand toward me.

"*Do you happen to know where the volunteer housing is on Gonen?*"

"Yeah, we will take you there. We are volunteers on the Kibbutz. Who are you?"

"*My name is Marty.*"

"What brings you to Gonen?"

"*While on the Greek Island of Ios, I was told by some friends that Gonen was the best Kibbutz in Israel.*"

Story 20: Jerusalem, Jerusalem

"Your friends are right. This is the best Kibbutz in Israel if you are a hippie volunteer on your way to India."

I could not believe my ears. How in the world could they possibly know I was headed to India? *"Who said anything about going to India?"*

"Most everyone who volunteers at Gonen is on their way to India."

"Why is that?"

"Because the Hippie Trail from Europe to India runs right through Israel; that is, if you are smart. And being Jewish helps."

"Why is Israel such a good stopping off place for those on the Hippie Trail?"

"Hippies come to Gonen to get healthy on free medical and all the healthy food you can eat. It is a good idea to put on a few pounds before heading to India."

"That does make perfect sense. And do they stop off at the Kibbutz on their return from the East?"

"You are a quick study. Yes, many return here after getting sick in India. As a matter of fact, some return looking as if they are about to die."

"Oh, that would be bad. Very bad, actually."

"Anyone who goes on to India really needs to have their act together, or suffer the consequences. More than one hippie has died in India."

I could hardly believe my ears. My plan to fake my death in India sounded better than ever. My new friends led me to the volunteers' housing area, where I met some of the other volunteers. I could hardly wait to get settled into my new digs. There were twelve little cabins—more like really old cottages—of various sizes. I found and moved into one of the smaller unoccupied cabins.

The view from the dining room of the kibbutz was spectacular. To the north I could see the hills of Lebanon. Down the middle of the valley was the road to Damascus. To the northeast I could see Mount Hermon with a crown of snow upon its nine thousand feet high dome.

The first two weeks I worked on the Kibbutz, I picked apples. Kibbutz Gonen was a very diverse agricultural community, with beef cattle; dairy cows; alfalfa fields; apple, orange, and avocado groves; a variety of melons and berries; and all sorts of vegetables. The food was great, and all you could eat. It was actually better than I had envisioned. I really enjoyed the Israelis and the kibbutz lifestyle. The only major issue I had with the Kibbutz is that we had to work six days out of each week.

However, there was a custom that I really liked at the end of the workweek, on Friday nights. It was called Shabbat-Shalom. Everyone would clean up from the day of work and put on something nice; that is, if you happened to own something nice looking. The tables in the massive dining room were all decked out with special things, and each table setting was aglow with candlelight. I did happen to notice that every table had a bottle of wine on it.

There were only six to eight people at each table. Some of the Israelis didn't drink wine, and others only drank a little with their meal. The volunteer workers drank more wine than the Israelis. I learned quickly that it was appropriate to take a partially consumed bottle of wine from another table if the Israelis had left the table after the meal. At night's end, there were several bottles of wine left on not a view tables.

At my third Shabbat-Shalom meal, I happened to notice a good number of bottles that hardly had any wine taken from them. After consuming a great deal of wine, it occurred to me that I should take a few of the bottles back to my little cabin. It was late November, and it was a cold night. I had worn my very large, baggy trench coat. It had big pockets on the inside, and on the outside.

I filled those pockets with as many bottles of wine as I could carry. I even put a couple down my coat sleeves. All in all, I was able to conceal six bottles of red wine. Many of the Israelis had already left the second-story dining room, and nobody was really paying much attention to what the volunteers were doing. I thought that was the perfect time to make my way over to the huge staircase that led to the ground-floor entrance.

Carefully, I started down the staircase. You could hear the bottles clanging together as I took each step. I don't know what happened, but in

Story 20: Jerusalem, Jerusalem

a flash, I was tumbling head over heels down the staircase. When I landed on the floor at the bottom of the staircase, I quickly got up to inspect the damage of broken bottles, and possibly physical injury to myself.

I opened the long coattails to see if there was any shattered glass or blood. But to my amazement, I had not broken one bottle. I looked up and saw at least two-dozen Israelis hanging out in the nearby foyer. They had all turned toward me to see what was gong on. I was busted for sure. Then, in a spontaneous roar of cheers and applause, they gave me a standing ovation. I took a few bows, and then stumbled back to my cabin. I really liked the kibbutz Israelis. They were hardworking, fun-loving people.

After a few weeks, I made my first trip to the Old City of Jerusalem, on the back of a BMW motorcycle owned by a Danish friend I had met at Kibbutz Gonen. I went to the café that John Griggs had directed me to go to in order to meet the Palestinian contact. I was surprised that he was actually at the café. We sipped mint tea, and exchanged stories about the Brotherhood, and adventures he had dealing drugs in Israel.

I traded him fifty tabs of Orange Sunshine LSD for a few ounces of Lebanese hashish. Bringing hashish back to the volunteers at Gonen was a very good way to assure your status and ongoing popularity. I returned two more times to the Old City to do business with the Palestinian. From what I could see, he ran most of the serious drug dealing in the Old City of Jerusalem.

I had discussed at length with him the possibility of selling a large amount of LSD. We would sip hot mint tea, discussing the details of the deal for painfully long periods of time. I could never understand why they drank hot tea from a glass instead of a coffee cup or mug. I found it an utterly strange custom. I was trying to move slowly with him and his organization, mainly because their culture and ways seemed so strange and foreign to me.

At our third meeting, he showed me a stack of US hundred dollar bills, to convince me that he could handle a large deal. We set the date of the deal for the upcoming Shabbat-Shalom. I only got Saturdays off from the Kibbutz. We were to meet on Friday night, December 23, at a local nightclub, just outside the Damascus Gate of the Old City of Jerusalem.

When I returned one week later, I couldn't help but think what a great Christmas this would be, after doing this last deal before heading off to Bombay, India. The thousands of dollars I would make from this deal would be enough greenbacks to buy 180 pounds of Afghan hashish, with plenty left over for expenses.

There would be a lot of traveling expenses. I would need to pay the doctor to falsify my death. It would be costly to have a first-class fake passport and supporting ID made for me. I'd have housing and food expenses while I waited for all my efforts to return in the form of many thousands of those greedy greenbacks from the good ole USA.

The hashish, once delivered in my pretend coffin to the States, would be worth well over two hundred thousand dollars. The mule carrier who would bring the money to me in India would become my partner. We would have more than enough to have a sailboat built for us in Goa, India, with over a thousand pounds of Afghan hashish pounded into the keel. The Brotherhood would supply the crew for the sailboat, as it had done a few times before. I tried to imagine what it would be like to sail across the Pacific Ocean to Maui, Hawaii. I would be wealthy beyond anything I had thought possible.

John Griggs, my neighborhood friend and chieftain of the Brotherhood, had made me a promise. If the hashish in my coffin proved successful, and if I pulled off the scam with a hash-packed sailboat keel, he would cut me in on the Brotherhood's "last dance," as he called it. The last dance of the Brotherhood was to buy an island somewhere in the South Pacific, and just disappear in paradise lost.

Story 20: Jerusalem, Jerusalem

I fantasized about all the adventure and possibilities of sailing across the South Pacific en route to Maui. The reality that I was facing a thirty-year prison sentence back in the States seemed a million miles away.

The Friday night Shabbat-Shalom had finally arrived. My Danish friend gave me a ride on his BMW motorcycle to the bus station of Kiryat Shmona. I bought a bus ticket to the Old City of Jerusalem. At long last, I was on the bus, and on the road from the Golan Heights of northern Galilee to Jerusalem. I wanted to use public transportation, just in case there might be a police checkpoint along the road to Jerusalem.

I arrived early to check into a crummy old hotel a few minutes from the ancient biblical city of Old Jerusalem. After settling into the crappy hotel room, I decided to get a bite to eat before meeting with the Palestinian dealer. I headed for the Old City, and walked through the Damascus Gate, looking for a place to eat.

I returned to the little café in the Muslim sector. All the eateries of the Jewish sector were closed for Shabbat-Shalom. After a highly questionable bowl of some oddly eatable mystery mush and a few glasses of mint tea, it was time to be off to meet the Palestinian dealer at the prearranged nightclub location.

Break on Through to the Other Side

Marty pondering impending drug deal in Israel

Story 21:
To Die or Not to Die?

Who you say you are is not how others
will see or remember you.
Your actions will bring into focus your lasting image.
—Uncle Bear

As I walked back to the Damascus Gate, everyone I saw looked like they had escaped from the set of a Fellini film. I had a very strange, uneasy feeling in the pit of my stomach, but convinced myself that it was probably the food I had just eaten.

It took me ten minutes to walk to the Arab nightclub for our meeting. The music was extremely loud and annoying in the club. It was some kind of weird-sounding Middle East rock and roll. The strobe lights were blinding and irritating.

I tried to look for my Palestinian dealer/contact in the smoky room. I could hardly make out anyones face, but I could hear someone calling out, "My friend! My friend, over here."

I could not tell where in the club the voice was calling from. Finally, I saw what appeared to be someone across the room waving his arms in the air back and forth. It was the Palestinian dealer.

I thought, *What an idiot, yelling and waving his arms—nothing like doing serious business in private.* I walked across the dance floor toward his table, and heard the words, "Yes, my friend, you have found me. Please have a seat and join me."

I sat down, and we talked while sharing a mixture of tobacco and hashish in a hookah pipe. The top of my head felt like it was going to blow off from the tobacco. I hadn't smoked cigarettes in two years, but I didn't want to offend the Palestinian dealer by rejecting his pipe. I quickly ordered a cold beer to settle my raw throat and help calm my nerves.

"*Do you have the money with you that we previously agreed upon?*"

"Yes, of course, what else would you think?"

"*Is the cash in US one hundred dollar bills?*"

Irritated by my question, he answered, "Yes! Why do you ask me such things?"

He reached inside his trench coat, and pulled out a big wad of US hundred dollar bills. He held the stack of bills in his left hand, and with the thumb of his right hand, he bent the bills and flipped through them, showing me that indeed they were all US one hundred dollar bills.

I forced a smile and replied, "*I just wanted to make sure we were on the same page.*"

"What does this mean, same page?"

I shook my head from side to side and said, "*It really doesn't matter. Let's do this deal.*"

"Yes, where is the LSD?"

I opened my backpack and encouraged him to look inside, to see that I indeed had several thousand tabs of Orange Sunshine. He looked inside the bag and said, "We must count, I must count."

I replied in utter shock and disbelief, "*You want to count each tab of Orange Sunshine? There are a few thousand tabs of LSD.*"

"Yes, of course. I must count them before I can give you money."

"*Where in the world do you plan on counting them?*"

"I have safe place to count, and I have driver in alley waiting for us."

I did not like the idea, to say the least, but I wanted that money so badly. I had become desperate to get the money and get on with my new life in India. I nodded my head, and reluctantly agreed to go with him.

Story 21: To Die or Not to Die?

He smiled broadly, and picked up my backpack from the table, saying, "Yes, let us go count, and then you get your money. I promise."

We got up from the table, and I followed him out the back door of the nightclub. As he had said, a car with a driver and the engine running was waiting for us in the alley.

The dealer opened the front passenger door for me, and motioned for me to get in. I started to enter the car, but before my butt hit the seat, I felt a hand grab me by the collar of my coat, and with a forceful jerk, I was thrown backward to the ground. The dealer quickly jumped into the front seat with my backpack and the LSD.

Reacting with unexpected speed, I leapt to my feet and thrust myself after the deceiver. I caught him with both hands. My right hand grabbed the lapel of his coat, and my left hand clutched at the throat of his turtleneck sweater.

Within a moment, I was holding onto the dealer with a death grip. He was holding onto the open car door with his left hand, and with his right hand he grasped to get a firm hold of the front seat of the car. The driver had put the pedal to the metal. In a split second, I was jerked off my feet; only my two hands clutching his coat and sweater kept me from being separated from these evil bastards.

I was being ripped off! They had my LSD, and I didn't have their money. I could hear the tires squeal as the car roared down the alleyway. I was being dragged by the car, with only the grasp of my hands keeping me from smashing face first into the pavement. He screamed something in Arabic as he strained to keep his grip on the open car door and the front seat.

My body, from the right hip, thigh, and knees downward to my dangling legs and feet, scraped and bounced against the pavement. The car sped faster and faster. Yet everything seemed to be moving in slow motion. Words fail me to describe the horror that filled my heart. I knew I was about to die. I had the impression I was suspended over the chasm of an endless abyss. Spontaneously, memories flared in full color snapshots; my life was flashing before me. I knew it was only a matter of time before I would no longer be able to hang on. I knew I would die when my head would inevitably be smashed into the pavement.

No way in the world could I have prepared myself for a moment like this, nor would I have ever even tried to prepare myself for this experience, my impending death. Out of my heart came these feeble words, *Father, I know I'm about to die, and I know that I'm going to hell, but could I just see Jesus before I go to hell?*

Story 22:
Does the "I Am" Care?

*Miracles, by their very nature, break the laws of nature.
Simply put, the impossible enters the world of the possible,
where miracles are so natural.*
—Uncle Bear

Father, I know I'm about to die, and I know that I'm going to hell, but could I just see Jesus before I go to hell? The very moment those words made their way out of my hardened heart, I felt a euphoric calm. It was the presence of the Presence.

I can't explain the moment in human terms of translation or interpretation. I didn't know what I knew until I knew what I didn't know. I just knew in my knower that the Eternal One was now on the scene. All I can say is, when *I Am* shows up at a moment like this, you know it!

The next thing that held my awareness was that I did not seem to have any bodily weight. I felt like the wind, like a feather in the breeze. Within this awesome Presence, it was as though time had stopped, or there was no time. There was only the present, only the moment I was experiencing.

My grip was now more than enough to pull me onto the front seat. To this day, I do not know if I pulled myself into the car, or if the Eternal One lifted me up and put me on the front seat. Within split seconds, the driver slammed on the brakes. I believe he felt the presence of the Presence, too, but in a very bad way.

Break on Through to the Other Side

The would-be getaway car screeched to a halt in the alley. I was now on top of the dealer, in the front seat, still grasping him with both of my hands. We were face to face. He looked terrified, and I think I had a similar look on my face. The Holy One had just saved my life!

I slowly got up from being on top of my would-be killer. I stood up next to the car, with the dealer still in my frozen grasp. I think I was still holding onto him mainly out of shock that the Eternal One had just saved my life. I don't remember how long we both stood there, looking into each other's terrified eyes.

Finally, the dealer broke the standoff by butting me in the face with his forehead. He broke my nose, and I let go of him. He jumped back into the front seat, and the driver pressed down on the gas pedal. They sped away as originally planned, but now I didn't care that they had ripped me off.

I had just been dangled over the abyss for a few seconds—and that was enough to change my perspective, my direction, and my life forever. I was in some kind of cosmic daze. Through the shock of facing certain death and being saved from it, a transformation had just taken place within my spirit, my being.

I don't remember how I found my way back to the hotel room. I do remember flushing all the remaining drugs in my possession down the toilet in my hotel room. I was bewildered by the strange calmness and peace that had come over me. I felt like I didn't have a care in the world.

I actually lay in bed and giggled out loud continually in what appeared to be waves of insanity. I did wonder if I had completely lost my mind. I also wondered if the peace I was experiencing was like being in the eye of a hurricane. I felt as if I was floating in a huge batch of warm, soothing Swiss chocolate. Finally, without anger or fear, I fell asleep.

The next morning, I woke up feeling refreshed and alive. I took a bus back to Kibbutz Gonen and stayed there for three days. On the morning of the third day I borrowed my Danish friends motorcycle and went to Mt. Hermon. I rode the motorcycle as high on the mountain as the dirt road would take me. I climbed up the mountain with a friend

Story 22: Does the "I Am" Care?

in search of the headwaters of the Jordan River. There I renewed my covenant with the Holy One.

Early the next day I caught a ride with an Israeli from the Kibbutz who was picking someone up at the Tel Aviv airport. The strange peace I had experienced the days before was still upon me. I was starting to wonder if the I Am had rewired my brain. I felt that my new life had some kind of purpose, unknown though it might be.

I canceled my ticket to Bombay, and bought a ticket to Switzerland. I flew to Geneva the next day. After arriving, I hitchhiked back to the University of the New World in Haute-Nendaz, and bought a VW bus from one of the students who was leaving for New York.

The VW bus already had a makeshift platform bed built into it, so it was kind of a bed on wheels. Most of the students I had previously met had left the would-be university. The local Swiss police had arrested a couple of them for dealing drugs, and that pretty well finished it for the remaining hippies.

I drove that dark green VW bus through the Alps, from one mountain area to another. I didn't know what to do. All I really knew was that my Eternal Father had saved me from dying in some back alley of Jerusalem. For the most part, I spent my days hiking in one mountain area after another in the Swiss Alps, calling out to the I Am. On many occasions, I sang new songs of whatever words lifted out of my heart and through my vocal chords.

My theme was a constant flow of thanking the Eternal One for love, forgiveness, presence, kindness, peace, joy, and so on. The list grew, and surpassed all I had ever known or believed. Although I did ask for help from time to time regarding my future, I spent countless hours walking and hiking, simply thanking the One for everything. It had taken a near-death experience to have a genuine spiritual breakthrough to the other side. I now knew what it was like to be on the other side, truly experiencing the Eternal Being in the here and now.

On one of my spirit walks on an absolutely beautiful day, I walked upward on a hiking trail for nearly three hours, without a break. I had grown weary, and needed to stop for a rest. I saw what looked to be a huge pine tree just ahead of me, only a few feet off the trail. The old pine tree, with its enormous lower branches, beckoned me to come and rest. I wondered how many decades this magnificent tree had been standing silently alone.

The powerful, proud pine was surrounded by tall, uncut green grass. I made myself comfortable under the pleasant tree, in the wonderfully soft grass. While gazing across the springtime lush green valley below, a poem began to birth itself in my thoughts. I quickly wrote down the words:

> *The humble gentle sacrificial blades of grass leaning in support*
> *beneath me simply said, Welcome Seer, sit and rest...Selah.*
> *Green with your ever-changing hues*
> *Green with your fondness for new life*
> *Green with yet unnumbered tones*
> *Green, the nurturer of the weary*
> *Green, the gift of peace to the lonely eye*
> *Green, the restorer of strength*
> *Green, the beacon of live and let live*
> *Green, the emerald stone of my birth*
> *Green, the isle of my heritage*
> *Green, the eyes of my true love*
> *Green, in all your glory, I embrace you.*

From the transcendence of my inner knower—through my childlike poetic metaphor—I knew that the eyes of my true love would be green. I continued to sit with perfect pleasure in silence, as the present was completely satisfying to me. I don't know how long the blissfulness lasted, given the absence of awareness of the space-time continuum. I was in complete peace inside the cocoon of the present moment.

Story 22: Does the "I Am" Care?

An eagle flying high above me caught my eye. In an instant, my brain began to examine the majesty of the powerful bird, and the chatter of my brain began once again. I was no longer in the cocoon of the present moment. I was somewhat disappointed that my mind had pulled me back into clock time. Yet, I was deeply grateful for the exuberant presence I had experienced in the eternity of now.

There was, however, a wonderful feeling of awareness and peace that passed beyond my understanding. A gentle smile had found a home on my face. I began to chuckle, and then laugh out loud for no apparent reason—until my thoughts chimed in once again with useless information: *Marty, you know you might be losing your mind.* This uninvited observation only made me laugh louder.

I confronted my thoughts, and spoke to them, "*You are not the best of me; you only think you are. The I Am at the center of my being is much, much better than you could ever be.*"

My chattering thoughts went silent for a few—very few—minutes, and then wanted to get in the final word. *Well, Marty, at least we now know the love of your life has green eyes.*

I laughed again, and agreed with my thoughts. "*Yes, you are correct; she will have green eyes.*"

I stood to my feet without effort, and spoke, "*OK, everybody, let's move on with our walk. Body, soul, and spirit: are you ready to go?*"

The chatter of my mind spoke up once again, *Why don't you say, body, mind and spirit?*

Because you think you are running the show, and I want to remind you in any way I can that you are not the boss. I want you to realize that you are a function, like my ears or eyes. You always try to overstep your thoughts—to think it is all about you—but you are wrong. You are subject to my soul and spirit. So! You might as well get use to it.

Break on Through to the Other Side

Marty at the Headwaters of the Jordan River, Israel

Story 23:
Springtime

Hope is a pleasant companion who holds your hand,
while your other hand reaches into the future,
free of the gravity of the moment,
to bring back a dream for the waiting, waking world to see.
—Uncle Bear

The Holy Eternal One never promised days without pain, laughter without sorrow, or sun without rain. But the One has empowered us with strength for today, comfort for the tears, and light for the way. If the I Am brings you to it, the One will bring you through it. We are equipped with the ability to learn to embrace change—even learn to love it—for change is the only thing that is certain. It has been said that if your present location feels like hell, just keep on moving.

Live each day as if it were the most important day of your life, because it may be your last, or at least as you have previously known it. In mystical, paradoxical truth, today *is* your last day, because tomorrow *is* perpetually, eternally out of reach, and yesterday does not exist. It *is* gone forever. All you will ever have or lose *is* now.

Springtime did smile and shine on me early that year. There were many cold nights before spring came when I wondered if I would wake up on earth or in heaven. With a down coat, down comforter and down pillow, I was really getting "down" in those days. Yet, despite the cold days and colder nights, I was filled with joy and an ongoing peace like I had never experienced before.

Being dangled over the abyss has a remarkable effect on the gratefulness meter of your heart and soul. I now seemed to appreciate everything and everyone. Somehow, in my spirit, I knew that everything was going to be all right. I knew intuitively that my hopes—not my hurts—would now shape my future. I had become a friend of the Eternal One.

The One had not only saved my life from death and outer darkness, I think something of infinite value from the Spirit was imparted to me. It was a gift, and I believe this gift is available to anyone, and for everyone. I simply came to the end of my road, my way, and had inadvertently entered a place of a mystical rest and a profound relaxed trust in the Creator, the Redeemer, the Kind Power of the Universe, the Prince of Peace, the Three in One.

Jesus became more than cool to me. It was then I came to realize that Christ was not Jesus's last name. The Christ Spirit has been part of the Eternal One for all eternity. The mystery of the Three in One is beyond comprehension. It is, by design, beyond every human being's capacity to understand the infinite characteristics of the Creator, the I Am, the One. Yet we are given a glimpse of eternity and infinity every time we look up at the midnight sky or into the eyes of a newborn baby.

On one of my outings, I met a Christian hippie named Richard. He told me about a place where other hippies were welcomed into a community of believers. They were encouraged to engage, and even debate about religion and theology. Their opinions actually had a voice, and they were never told, "This is the correct theology, and you should just believe it." I was impressed. Richard could tell I was very interested in this commune, and asked if I wanted him to take me there. I did. We teamed up, and headed for this special place, called L'Abri.

Story 23: Springtime

It was a place like nothing I had ever heard of or seen before. Francis Schaeffer and his dear wife Edith were the sages who had founded the commune and made it their home into their elder years.

L'Abri was a touch of heaven, and I enjoyed the experience immensely. It was such a haven of rest for hippies who were searching for spiritual answers. I was worn out mentally, emotionally, and physically. Thoroughly and completely exhausted, I found temporary rest for my soul at L'Abri. Unfortunately, my stay there was short-lived.

Every room in all the chalets at L'Abri were filled to overflowing with temporary residents. There seemed to be new hippie visitors every day. On one glorious mid-April day, I was sharing a hearty Sunday brunch with Edith and Francis Schaeffer. They were such a delightful older couple, and it was so cool to be loved and accepted by these wonderful lovely people.

The topic of the overcrowded conditions came up during lunch. I volunteered to leave, because I was one of the only hippies there who owned a bed on wheels, my VW bus. I was kind of hoping they would ask me to stay, but it wasn't realistic—their housing was full to capacity. During our conversation, Edith, with her gentle, grandmotherly voice, asked, "Marty have you ever heard of Youth With A Mission?" I said I had never heard of it. She suggested that I might want to visit the YWAM school campus, which was only a couple of hours away by car.

It was mid-April, and in the air there was a chill; a few snowflakes were making one of their last appearances of the season as they floated to the earth. Still, spring was in the air, and new life seemed to be everywhere I looked.

I felt a bit like a homing pigeon as I directed my VW bus to the outpost of Chalet-à-Gobet in Lausanne, Switzerland, where Youth With A Mission had secured its international headquarters. I had never been to Lausanne before, but I sensed a touch of destiny in the air. The directions Francis Schaeffer had given me were very detailed and easy to understand—similar to the many extraordinary books he had written on Christian theology.

That very afternoon, I drove to Lausanne with three friends of mine who wanted to go with me. We threw our backpacks into my VW bus, and took off to discover YWAM. None of us had been to YWAM before, and we really had no idea what our Heavenly Father had in store for us. Within two hours, we arrived at the tiny parking lot of the old converted hotel YWAM had acquired. The new sign read, Youth With A Mission. It was YWAM's first permanent training center, as well as its international headquarters.

When I walked through the doors of the converted hotel into the foyer, I had the oddest feeling that I was coming home. It was one of those magical déjà vu, goose bump experiences. In fact, I had never been here before, but it felt like home—or at least what I imagined a home could feel like.

After entering the old hotel, we were greeted by several students, who welcomed us with big smiles and open arms. Love and acceptance resided in the occupants and in the very atmosphere of Chalet-à-Gobet. However, I must admit my shadow self did wonder cynically why they were being so nice. A defensive thought rolled through my head: *Maybe this is a cult?* It was hard for me to just accept love for what it was.

I was introduced to the school leader, Joe Portale, who asked, "What brings you to YWAM?"

I didn't know how to answer him, so I simply said, "*God, I think.*"

He then asked, "Do you have a place to stay in Lausanne?"

I smiled and answered, "*Here, I hope.*"

Joe laughed and said, "Here it is. You are more than welcome to stay here for a few days."

"*What if we would like to stay longer than a few days?*"

Joe grinned and said, "Well, we have just started our spring school. If you were to stay longer, you would need to be a student in the school."

STORY 23: SPRINGTIME

I looked at the three friends who had come with me. They were all nodding their heads and smiling, signifying a unified *yes!* Their bobbing heads reminded me of those silly dolls you can put on the dashboard of a car that bob up and down with the movement of the vehicle. After a momentary chuckle, I turned back to our generous host and said, "*Well, Joe, where do we sign up?*"

He hesitated, then said, "I will just need to check with the director, Loren Cunningham, to make sure that everything is OK with you joining the school. Would you like to join us for dinner while I find out?"

"*Yes! Of course we would.*"

By the time we were finished eating, Joe emerged with good news, "Yes, everything is fine, and you are welcome to stay for the spring school. When you are ready, I will show you to your rooms."

Show us to our rooms. I was shocked by the reception we were experiencing. It had been many moons since I'd had a place to hang my beret with peace and security. "*Joe, my brother, thank you so much.*"

After he had showed my three friends to the male and female dorms, he said, "Marty, your room is one floor up."

I thought, *Did he just say my room? My room!* I found it hard to believe my ears. I followed Joe up the staircase to the third floor. He walked to the end of the hall, opened a door, and said, "This will be your room." To say I was surprised and thoroughly blown away by being given my own private room would be a major understatement. Joe opened the door wider and said, "Welcome to your new home."

I did my best to hold back the tears in my eyes, and I simply said, "*Wow! This is so cool*", which kind of said it all.

Break on Through to the Other Side

Marty seeking the I Am in the mountains of Switzerland

Story 24:
Diversity & Harmony in Switzerland

*Diversity is the primary colors that blend into endless
shades and hues of delight to our eyes.
Diversity is the essential taste sensations, and the endless
combinations of savory pleasure.
Diversity is the key musical notes, and all the varied
arrangements to create endless melodies of enjoyment to the ear.
Diversity is the family of humankind, where no two are the same,
and all are unique beyond description, with each
having unsurpassable value.
Diversity in eternity is the Three in One,
and that we also may be One*
—Uncle Bear

I was more than surprised to receive my own private room, which had its own sink with hot and cold running water. It is amazing how much you can appreciate the simple things in life when you are in danger of losing them. The private room was perfect for my spiritual condition at the time. I did a lot of late-night reading and praying.

The next day, after I had moved into my new digs, it was arranged for me to meet with the Cunningham's. Loren and Darlene Cunningham were the founders of Youth With A Mission. Darlene was black and white in her approach to socializing and productivity. Loren was more laid-back in his leadership style, which worked well for me. He had the biggest grin I had ever seen. They both possessed an unusual charisma and magnetism.

After the first week of the school, I asked to meet again with Loren, mainly because of my earlier summer TV show experience. I had a few suggestions about how we could improve the videotaping of the lectures. Loren basically gave me the responsibility of taping all the classroom teachings from then on. He had an amazing disposition about releasing young people into leadership positions, without much concern for how we might screw things up.

Within two weeks of commencing school, I was more of a staff volunteer than a student. I really liked the opportunity, mainly because I had the afternoons free, which facilitated my daily walks with the I Am in the Swiss forest near the school. Usually I walked and prayed for three hours every afternoon. I cherished those afternoon walks with the Holy One.

It was during those walks that I learned to just be in the presence of the Presence. I found it rather addictive. I looked forward to those walks every day. Those were wonderful days in my life—getting right with the One. Because of my ordeal, and the lifesaving experience in Israel, I started a prayer time, every day right after lunch. We would pray every day for peace in the Middle East, Israel and Jerusalem.

No one ever asked me any details regarding my past. The topic just never came up. So I followed the advice of silence: I kept the past on the down low (the updated version of let a sleeping dog lie). However, one day, toward the end of the lecture phase of the school, the past came to haunt me.

That unforgettable day, I was sitting among the other students because I wasn't videotaping the session. Loren was sharing his vision regarding YWAM's international outreach at the upcoming Olympics to be held in Munich, Germany. He abruptly halted his emotionally charged exhortation.

Two Swiss policemen had appeared at the doorway of the lecture room. Loren hesitated, then in a meek voice asked the officers if he

Story 24: Diversity & Harmony in Switzerland

could assist them. One policeman remained at the door, and the other officer walked to Loren, his back to the classroom. He spoke a few words that I could not hear. In a quick motion, the policeman turned toward the students, and looked up and down each aisle. He was obviously looking for someone.

His eyes returned to the aisle I was sitting in, and he looked right at me. I thought, *Oh no, he is looking at me. I knew I shouldn't have stayed in one place as long as I have stayed here in the school. He is here to arrest me.* The officer squared his shoulders and placed his right hand on his holstered handgun. He started to walk with determination down the aisle I was sitting in.

I could feel the adrenaline rushing through my heart and head. My face must have turned red with fear and the impending embarrassment of being arrested in front of the entire school. When he came alongside me, I took a deep breath, and readied myself for the groan of despair I was about to make. But I heard his boot take a step past me—I held my breath. The policeman put his hand on the shoulder of the person sitting directly behind me.

The officer arrested him on the spot, and with his hand still on the guy's shoulder, guided him out of the room. I was now in a cold sweat, and must have looked terrified. Julie, sitting across from me in the next aisle, asked, "Marty, are you all right? You look like you just saw a ghost."

"*No, uh, no. I'm fine. I just hate to see anyone get arrested.*" I had almost completely lost it when the policeman had come down my aisle. Wow! What a relief it was to still be sitting in my seat, my crimes still unknown to those around me. My new friends, my peers, were still of the impression that I was one of them—well, at least for the present moment, anyway.

Loren was bulletproof. After leading us in a prayer for Jay, the one arrested, he went right back to sharing his vision about the upcoming outreach event at the Olympics. I think he was on autopilot, which gave us all some time to just sit there and compose ourselves after what had just taken place. I don't think any of us were listening with much concentration or focus.

Break on Through to the Other Side

Marty baptized by Loren Cunningham in Lausanne, Switzerland

Story 24: Diversity & Harmony in Switzerland

The following week some of the students wanted to be baptized in water. It was still early spring. Lake Geneva or any nearby river would be way too cold for a baptism. Someone suggested taking the old freestanding bath tub that was being stored in the shed and using it for the baptism. We carried the old tub out to the lawn area and filled it with water. It sat in the sun all morning and into the afternoon. I was baptized that sunny late afternoon by Loren Cunningham.

Two weeks before the spring school had concluded its three-month lecture phase, Loren Cunningham and Don Stephens came knocking at my door. When I answered the door, I was genuinely surprised to see them standing there. Loren spoke up and said, "Marty, we would like for you to pray about taking a group of students from this school to Israel, and start a YWAM base of operation in Israel."

I was very touched that they would ask me to do such a thing. But I knew it would not be possible for me to lead anyone anywhere. It was now time for me to open up and tell them about my past. For several seconds, I thought about what I should say, while they stood there in silent anticipation waiting for an answer. "*Well, Loren, I am currently facing a thirty-year sentence for conspiracy to overthrow the United States government.*"

A painfully long silence followed my confession. Loren and Don just stood there looking at each other. Don had a sheepish half grin on his face, and Loren just plain looked like a deer staring into headlights. Finally, Loren responded, "Well, I guess it's just not God's timing."

With that ambiguous comment, they slowly retreated from my doorway, and gently closed the door. Loren never brought up the subject again.

Break on Through to the Other Side

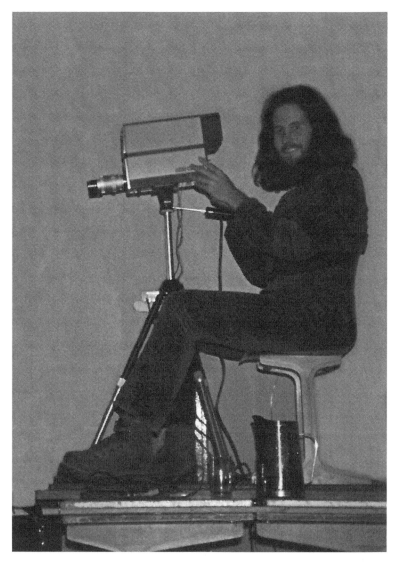

Marty video taping at YWAM Lausanne

Story 25:
One for All & All for One

*Christ the Creator breathed life into the first living soul,
and now that breath of life is shared equally with every
human being on earth, regardless of race, color, creed, or religion.
We all breathe the same air, the breath of life.*
—Uncle Bear

All my fellow students were praying about where they would be going for the two-month field trip phase of the school. Obviously, Israel was out of the question for me. However, I kind of thought the rest of Europe was a reasonable possibility.

I prayed and fasted on water only for a solid week. The school nurse noticed me looking gaunt and stumbling a bit. She demanded that I curtail my fast with at least orange juice. I prayed on for another week, but there was no answer from the One.

Everyone else was getting direction as to where they would be going for the summer. Most of them believed they were receiving inspiration to go to Munich, Germany, to do advance prep work for the upcoming Summer Olympics to be held there.

All my prayers seemed to be bouncing off an iron curtain and steel ceiling. For the life of me, I could not get a clear sense of the presence of the Presence. I was a bit sheepish and feeble in my toned-down approach to the Holy One. It finally occurred to me that the I Am was infinitely secure, and thoroughly able to handle any rants or rage I might throw in His direction.

I stepped up my prayer technique to one of highly charged, emotional interaction with the Eternal One. It was more like a one-sided debate. I yelled, stomped, threw my arms up into the air, and flat out got crazy with God. I demanded to know what the Creator wanted me to do regarding the two-month outreach. But I could not get the I Am to answer me.

One fine day, while having a heated discussion with myself, I blurted out these words. "*Marty, are you completely out of your mind? Do you think you can twist the arm of the Almighty to do what you want Him to do?*"

Then, into my mind, came these words: "Be still, and know that I Am."

I agreed to just hang out in the presence of the Presence regarding the direction of my field trip. I made a commitment to stop trying to get the Holy One to do what I wanted, when I wanted. A few days went by, and I was taking my afternoon prayer walk with the Beloved. I was just being in the moment, not asking for anything and thanking God for anything, when out of nowhere—or, should I say from everywhere—came this undeniable impression upon my consciousness. It was so simple and clear: "Stay in Lausanne."

The awareness was complete and comprehensible in just three words, without any explanation or interpretation. However, my peace of mind did not last very long. As I walked back toward Chalet-à-Gobet, I first thought about what I should eat after fasting for nearly three weeks. Then my thoughts began to wander, and the old chatter of mindless discussion began, ever so effortlessly, in my head.

Spontaneously, I began to argue with myself. However, apparently no one was winning this neurotic internal debate. That was all my shadow self needed to turn the discussion toward the Almighty. Within minutes, my false self was back in the driver's seat, questioning the I Am, and what I believed the Creator had impressed upon my conscious awareness.

Story 25: One for All & All for One

Before I had any grasp of the situational slide of my unbelief, I blurted out a defiant question. *"Stay in Lausanne? Stay in Lausanne! Everyone else will be having the time of their lives on a two-month field trip all over Europe and North Africa."* To make matters worse, I asked the Eternal One a seriously complaining question: *"And what am I supposed to do in Lausanne for the next two months?"*

I really did not expect to hear an answer, but the rebuttal came swiftly, "Give of yourself to serve."

The mental defenses of my ego-driven, fallen self went to work immediately. *Marty, what are you thinking? They will have you cleaning toilets, washing dishes, and pulling weeds.* I argued with the Holy One for three days regarding this guidance. However, when all was said and done, I commanded my false self, my shadow self, to go back into the shadow land, where it belonged. I renewed my commitment to walk in the light of the Holy One, the light of my Beloved, the Word, the Truth.

I relinquished the ego-driven, self-proclaimed right to do what I wanted. I agreed with what I sensed was the leading of the Creator. I was to stay put at the school in Lausanne, and serve whatever needs arose or were asked of me. That was to be my two-month field trip. My selfish, self-centered ego was no longer in control.

I knew in my heart that if I were to leave with one of the other field trip teams, I would be in Big Daddy's metaphoric doghouse. Yet for the life of me, I could not understand why my Heavenly Father wanted me to stay in Lausanne for the next two months before the Olympics.

The time came for all the students to take off for their two-month field trip adventures. One of the teams even asked if they could use my VW bus, since I wasn't going anywhere. I grudgingly agreed to be generous.

I still remember standing in the parking lot of the school, waving good-bye to the last team to leave for their field trip. I was filled with a great deal of self-pity. I felt so alone and left behind. I felt abandoned by the God, and I did not understand why.

After a sleepless night of wrestling with the Holy One, I finally gave in again! I submitted to what I perceived to be the will of my Beloved

Creator. The next day, I showed up early to discover what my work duty would be. I was asked to paint the entire school entryway of the old hotel foyer.

I picked up a paintbrush and bucket of paint. I made a new commitment to have no self-pity, and to paint by faith. I was going to do the best job possible for the One, with all my heart. I declared a rallying commitment, and repeated it continually, "*One for All and All for One… One for All and All for One!*"

My rallying slogan was not original. I took it from the Three Musketeers motto, "All for one and one for all." I just put a new spin on it and gave it a little mystical life. After all, the One is for all of us and we in turn could all be for the One. I knew it was a little corny but it worked well regarding my attitude.

A week went by, then two weeks passed rapidly. I was being the best painter I knew how to be. But now, in my heart, I felt that the Creator was up to something. I really didn't know what that something was. I just knew in my inner knower that my Heavenly Father was not punishing or screwing with me, but had a plan with a purpose.

One fine sunny afternoon, I was high up on a very tall ladder, painting the ceiling of the main entry of the old hotel's foyer. To my surprise, a group of young people started pouring through the entry door. They were goofing around, laughing and talking while they passed very close to my ladder. A few of them actually passed right underneath me, walking between the outstretched legs of the ladder. Their inattentiveness was making me more than a little nervous; I was probably something like twelve feet off the ground.

There were at least two-dozen people I had never seen before. After a little bit of commotion with luggage and the normal stuff that accompanies a new group in a place they had never seen before, Darlene Cunningham greeted the new visitors. She gave them a general introduction to their surroundings, and their room locations.

Then I saw her. Wow! She was beautiful! I mean she was *really* beautiful. I was caught so off guard that I almost dropped my bucket of

Story 25: One for All & All for One

paint. I teetered on the ladder for a moment. She lit up the room with her smile. It was as if she had an actual glow about her.

She started to walk up the huge staircase to the higher floors. I had to say something, but what could I say? She was stunning. She was going upstairs. I had to say something. I had to get her attention. I panicked, and blurted out, "*Hey, yellow pants!*" *Hey, yellow pants? Had I really just said that?* Of course, it goes without saying, she was wearing really bright—I mean, *really* bright—yellow pants.

She leaned over the rail and looked down at me. She smiled. I could have passed out right there and then, but instead, I mumbled these dreadfully awkward words, "*So, yellow pants, where are you from?*"

She giggled and answered, "I'm from Southern California. Thousand Oaks."

I was so pleased that she noticed me, and that she was still smiling at me. "*How long are you going to be staying?*"

"Six weeks. We are going to be staying here six weeks."

I tried to hold in my feelings. I was about to explode with excitement. *Six weeks! She is going to be here with her college group for a month and a half.* I was completely stoked by the exciting good news. With childlike abandon, I wanted to throw my can of paint into the air.

I smiled back broadly, and simply said, "*Cool, that's very cool.*" My thoughts echoed in my head: *Oh yeah, it's going to be an interesting summer after all. Oh yeah, it is going to be a very interesting summer.*

Then a splendid thought occurred to me. *Was this the reason my Heavenly Father urged me to stay here at the school in Lausanne?* An old bible verse popped into my thoughts, "Hope is a wellspring of life for those who drink from it." I was totally wide open and thirsty for this kind of hope.

Break on Through to the Other Side

Marty & Mindy meet in Lausanne, Switzerland 1972

Story 26:
Honey & the Bear

*Meeting you was destiny. Getting to know you was magical.
But falling in love with you was beyond my restraint…
I knew I was a goner when being with you,
doing absolutely nothing, meant absolutely everything to me.*
—Uncle Bear

Our new guests wanted to check out the city of Lausanne. I volunteered to be their tour guide. I couldn't have asked for a better setup for my first night seeing her up close and personal.

They had rented a big van for their six-week stay in Switzerland. They had thought they were renting a Swiss hotel called Chalet-à-Gobet. They had no idea the facility had been converted into a private Christian school.

The time had come for the new arrivals to come downstairs and meet me in the parking lot. It was late June 1972, and the Swiss sun hung effortlessly in the sky, creating a warm golden glow. One by one, the new guests joined me in front of the former Chalet-à-Gobet hotel. But she, the special *she*, was not among them. I turned to enter the facility, to see if she might be hanging out in the foyer.

To my delight, there she was, the last one to exit the building. The setting sun illuminated her long blond hair. We were face-to-face, no more than two feet apart. The golden glow of the setting sun lit up her face and eyes—especially those green eyes. Her green eyes were soft and full of youthful beauty. I thought, *Her eyes are green! Those gorgeous eyes are green!* I wanted to kiss her right there and then. You could have knocked me over with a feather.

I tried to gather my thoughts and steady my emotions, so I could function as the group's host. When everyone got loaded into the van, I introduced myself, and asked their names. I really only wanted to hear one name. When she said her name was Mindy, I paused for a moment, and thought, *How far-out is this? Even her name is groovy.* I had never met a Mindy before. *Marty and Mindy. Wow, that sounds so right, so cool.*

As we drove into the old section of Lausanne, I couldn't help but hear some grumbling about the accommodations. They didn't have a clue when they arrived that this charming old Swiss hotel was actually the international headquarters for YWAM. There was no room service, no menus in the dining room, no housekeeping to make their beds every day.

To say the least, they were not very happy. This was not a Swiss hotel, as they had thought, but a Christian school. The school was in its field trip phase of the training. Only a handful of us were there, to hold down the fort and do a little refurbishing. I felt that maybe the Eternal One had set them up for much more than just the accommodations.

I had the opportunity that first night to turn some of their grumbling into a fun time, exploring the charming old parts of Lausanne. It was a clear, crisp night, and from the promenade we could see all the way across Lake Geneva to the shores of France.

I was enthralled and delighted by Mindy's presence and personality. Whatever it was that she possessed seemed to make anyone and everyone around her happy. I honestly could not keep my eyes off her. Simply put, I was drawn to her like a bear to honey. I had never experienced, as they say, love at first sight. But I sure did now. She was

Story 26: Honey & the Bear

absolutely beautiful in my eyes, and the best was yet to come. I learned in the days to follow something far more important. She was even more beautiful on the inside.

The next day, I met Mindy's father and mother in the dining room. I tried to make a good first impression. They were both approachable and enjoyable to talk with. Dr. Rawlins was very outgoing, confident, and friendly. Betty Rawlins was pleasant in her mannerisms, and was a well-crafted listener. She was kind, and had a royal-like demeanor about her.

Over the next few weeks, I spent as much time as humanly possible with Mindy. Our favorite venture together was to prepare a picnic and explore the nearby meadows and streams. Our fondness for each other grew so very naturally.

On one of our picnic outings, we came across a homeless person who was living in the forest in a makeshift covering made of tree limbs. When we greeted him, he immediately stood to his feet, and appeared dreadfully nervous.

Mindy quickly responded by saying, "Finally, we have found you. Here is the picnic we have prepared for you."

He mumbled a few incoherent words, and then in broken English, simply said, "Thank you—God bless you."

"You are very welcome, and can we do anything else for you?" Mindy asked.

"Swiss francs?" he replied.

"Yes! I'm sure we do." Then she looked at me with one of those "well, what are you going to do?" kind of looks.

"*Oh, yes. I have some Swiss francs I can give you.*" I pulled out my wallet and opened it.

Mindy said, "That will work perfectly." She then took the twenty Swiss francs from my wallet, and gave it to him.

We didn't have a picnic that day, but I was rewarded with a warm, soft kiss. I had most definitely fallen in love with Mindy.

Break on Through to the Other Side

Did I secretly and selfishly want her to want me? Absolutely! She was the first person in my life who had completely knocked me off my feet, and I liked it. I was in love, hook, line, and sinker.

Unfortunately, everything was not all it seemed to be. One day toward the end of Mindy's stay in Switzerland, we were slowly walking hand in hand in Lausanne. Out of nowhere, she mentioned something about going back to high school. I was in shock. I abruptly asked, *"How old are you?"*

She shyly whispered, "I'm sixteen."

"Sixteen!" "You are only sixteen?" I was dumb struck. I didn't know what to say, or how to say it. I felt embarrassed, and somewhat misled. *"But you are in the college group, attending classes with them."*

A little put off by my tone, she replied, "Yes, I am taking the college classes, and the credits go toward my high school graduation. I will actually be graduating a year early, at the end of this summer."

The emotions of shock, disbelief and bewilderment overcame me. I didn't know what to do or say. I was twenty-three, and an old twenty-three at that. We didn't talk much the rest of that evening. I was being a jerk—a common occurrence among young men from time immemorial.

When we got back to Chalet-à-Gobet, I went to my room and began to pray. I prayed and prayed and prayed that night. Yet, when all was said and done, I believed more strongly than ever that Mindy was the girl my Heavenly Father had chosen for me—and I don't mean just a girlfriend, but the love of my life and future wife!

I got down on my knees and prayed, *"Holy Father could you give me a little backing for what I believe you are speaking to my heart?"* Immediately, in my knower I heard these words in my thoughts: *Go to the Song of Songs.*

I knew exactly what that meant. I was to open my Bible to the book most commonly called the Song of Solomon. I quickly opened my Bible, and my eyes fell on this verse:

Story 26: Honey & the Bear

My beloved spoke and said to me,
Arise, my darling, my beautiful one,
come with me and see, the winter is past;
the rains are over and gone.
Flowers appear on the earth; the season of singing has come,
the cooing of doves is heard in our land.
The fig tree forms its early fruit; the blossoming vines spread their fragrance.
Arise, come, my darling; my beautiful one, come with me.
My dove in the clefts of the rock, in the hiding places on the mountainside.
Show me your face, let me hear your voice;
for your voice is sweet and your face is lovely.

That was all I needed to give me the courage to do what I knew I had to do the very next day. Sleep did not come easily for me that night.

I woke early the next morning; I thought it best to take a little prayer walk before breakfast. The main topic of my prayers related to what in the world I was going to say to Dr. Rawlins, Mindy's dad.

After my walk with the Eternal One, I went directly to the dining room. I saw Dr. Rawlins from across the room. I stood tall, squared my shoulders, walked over to Mindy's dad, and said, "*Dr. Rawlins, I am in love with your daughter. Do you think I am too old for her?*"

He paused for a moment, gathered his thoughts, and answered, "No, Martin, you are not too old for my daughter, but she is too young for you."

I wasn't disappointed with his answer. Frankly, I was impressed with his wit. I thought, *What an incredibly brilliant thing to say.* I actually took the answer as a half yes. I wasn't too old for her. She was just too young for me. The solution was doable—I just needed to wait until she was old enough for me.

Castle Chillon, Lake Geneva with Mindy's Dad - Dr. Rawlins

Betty Rawlins, the gentle and sensitive woman of God, had a secret. She had not made it known to anyone. Betty held the secret tenderly in her heart.

During breakfast, Dr. Rawlins told his wife that I had come to him before breakfast, to inform him that I was in love with his daughter. I had

Story 26: Honey & the Bear

previously told them most of the low points as to why I was hiding out in Europe. They knew I was facing a thirty-year sentence for conspiracy to overthrow the government of the United States.

Dr. Rawlins lightheartedly said, "When Marty told me he was in love with Mindy, I almost told him to take a number and stand in line." Mindy had received a bouquet of flowers sent to her in Switzerland from one of her admirers in California just a few days earlier. I was a long shot, at best. No, I was at best an extraterrestrial rocket launch into outer space.

Betty asked Duane if they could talk privately in their room. After breakfast, they went to their room, where Betty shared her secret with her husband.

"Duane, I believe God has put something very personal and important on my heart regarding Mindy."

"What kind of mysterious information has God given you?"

"I believe Marty is to be Mindy's life partner, Mindy's husband."

Dr. Rawlins was now obviously distraught, and pacing the floor. "Betty, you can't be serious. You know that Marty is facing a thirty-year sentence back in the States."

"Yes, Duane, I know what he has done and what he is facing. I'm just telling you, I believe Marty is God's choice for our daughter."

Dr. Rawlins was not all that pleased with what he was hearing, but he didn't think it would do any good to get in an argument with Betty over the matter. He was convinced, or at least hoped, that it was just puppy love, and would only last for the summer.

In my mind, it was a done deal, but I did have a monkey on my back. Well actually, it was more like a gorilla. I was facing a thirty-year sentence back in the United States.

I would be lying if I were to say I did not have some very real and serious doubts whether Mindy would actually be able to wait for me while I served my sentence. Was it even fair to ask her to wait for me?

Break on Through to the Other Side

Lovely ladies: Mindy and Mom - Betty Rawlins

Story 27:
Summer Olympics

When you find yourself emotionally discouraged,
in a gloomy state of mind,
Motion is the action required to change your emotion.
Sitting on your emotion will only expand your problem.
Your emotion can be altered by motion. Simply put—move!
—Uncle Bear

Mindy's Journal Entry: July 1972

It was a beautiful warm summer day when Marty and I climbed the ancient steps of Chillon Castle. We lingered at a vantage point overlooking Lake Geneva, with the French Alps in the distance. As we held each other close, we prayed together, and made a commitment before God, to love each other for the rest of our lives.

After our six weeks of summer love, it was now time for me to return home to the United States. With tears and sadness in leaving, Marty gently held me near, and whispered in my ear, *Read this on the plane home.* He then slipped a folder into my hands.

I could not wait; I opened it within minutes of our van driving away down the highway. In the folder were pressed flowers and a poem he had written for me.

Oh—You flower of many meadows
Your youth in fragrance and green eyes

Break on Through to the Other Side

Have led me beside still waters
And I resting in you, take care of me
Longing for comfort and a home
Birth pains and new life are strong
Heal me if you can, I'm missing a rib.

The day I had dreaded finally came. Mindy left with her family, along with the entire college group. They were on their way back to California. I could only look forward to letters for God only knew how many weeks, months, or maybe even years.

Within hours of her departure, I already missed her deeply. In the pit of my stomach, I felt an empty aching. Her parting gentle, soft kiss would need to last for a long, very long, time in my lovesick memory.

I prayed and asked my Heavenly Father if it was time for me to return to the United States and turn myself in to the authorities. I sensed through inner peace and a sort of intuition that I was just supposed to stay put. I didn't need any encouragement not to return to the States and turn myself in. I knew that my Heavenly Father had forgiven me, but I also knew that the FBI was not so forgiving.

However, I did continue to seek the voice of the Holy One. I asked, *"What then shall I be doing with myself in the meantime?"*

The answer seemed to echo in my inner thoughts, "Go to the Olympic Games."

My response was immediate and direct. I simply said, *"Groovy! Very groovy."*

Because of my video experience with my own rinky-dink TV show and the videotaping I had been doing for the school, I was asked the very next day to be on the three-man film crew from YWAM Lausanne for the Munich Olympics. I viewed this opportunity as a serious confirmation of Spirit's natural guidance.

The Olympic Outreach was YWAM'S first major international gathering for a specific outreach. I think something like a thousand young people showed up for it. I felt it was a personal honor to be on the

Story 27: Summer Olympics

three-man film crew. Roy Williamson, who headed up the team, had received an Emmy for his filming of the Soviet invasion of Hungary in 1956.

It was very cool working with him. However, he was, in my words, *a little crazy*. Ron had no fear of what or where he filmed. As the Olympic torch was making its final hand-off to the last person, who would run into the Munich Stadium, we were standing behind one of the roped-off areas on the street leading into the stadium.

Out of nowhere, he said to me, "When I move, you move! No questions and no hesitation, you are my sound for the film. You are connected to me like an umbilical cord. Whatever you do, do not kill the baby, and this film is the baby."

I simply nodded my head in bewildered agreement.

Before I could count to three, he grabbed the rope, lifted it over his head, and we were off. He quickly moved to the center of the street, with me following as closely as possible. He got down on one knee and went live. We were rolling film, and the sound was recording.

The torchbearer was only twenty feet away, and running right at us. He had the right of way—after all, he was the torchbearer for the Olympic Games of 1972. Roy just kept the film rolling. I could hear a number of policemen yelling at us in German, but I knew what they were saying. They were demanding and commanding us to get out of the way of the torchbearer.

I was ready to drop the boom microphone and head for the sidelines. I did not want to get arrested again in Germany. We held our ground in the center position of the street. The torch-bearer was within three strides of running into us. We held our ground, and I braced for the collision. At the last split second, the runner sidestepped us, and avoided an international incident.

However, the police were not pleased with us, or impressed with our photojournalism efforts. Once again, I felt that unmistakable tug of a German policeman grabbing me and escorting me to the sidelines, where we were supposed to be standing.

Break on Through to the Other Side

Roy just kept shouting, "American News! ABC! American News."

Another German police officer came up to us and said, in perfect English, "Are you that stupid? Do you know you could have been shot with rubber bullets for your antics? Do you have any idea how hard it is for the runner to see directly in front of himself at ground level? He is holding a big flame in front of his face. I should arrest you, but I won't, in the spirit of the games, the Olympic Games of Munich, Germany. We do not want any incident that will blemish our Olympics."

We apologized, and thanked the officer for his kindness and understanding, then quickly removed ourselves from the premises. Roy bought me a pint of beer for standing with him under the pressure of the moment.

From the Olympics, it was about an hour's drive to the YWAM facilities at Schloss Hurlach. The YWAMers simply called it the castle. YWAM leaders, Dave Boyd and Gary Stephens, had acquired the castle in the spring of 1972. It hosted something like one thousand young people who had come for the Olympic Outreach.

The outreach was going really well, until the unthinkable happened. Eight Palestinian terrorists murdered eleven Israeli Olympians. It was a national tragedy for Israel, and a national disgrace for Germany. The beautiful, dynamic international unity of the games came to a bloody halt, and the games were suspended.

On September 7, YWAM was given permission by the German authorities to hold a peace march through the city of Munich. Thousands of flowers were donated for the peace march. It would be the last *flower child* event I would ever participate in.

Oddly enough, when we began to film the start of the peace march, Roy said to me, "Marty, I think you should be in the march today." I handed my sound boom to the other assistant, and joined the front line of the march. We passed out thousands of flowers that day, and tried our best to represent the *Prince of Peace*.

On September 8, the games resumed, with the blessing of the nation of Israel. Five bodies of the Palestinian assassins were delivered

Story 27: Summer Olympics

to Libya, where they received hero's funerals and were buried with full military honors. I found their behavior disgusting, at best.

Of all the Islamic and Arab nations of the world, only one ruler spoke out against the atrocity. King Hussein of Jordan condemned the murders as unspeakable acts of violence. He was a very brave man for doing such a thing.

My Olympic venture, with all of its triumphs and the dark atrocities of the terrorists, was only a sign of the days ahead of us. The future of the modern world would hold bright, shining highs and grim, gruesome lows.

One of my brightest experiences at the end of the Olympics was the day I was asked to videotape an interview with Corrie Ten Boon. She was a legend in Europe for her courage during World War II. She and her Dutch family hid Jews in their home after the Nazi's invaded the Netherlands in 1940. The Jews were trying to escape the genocide perpetuated by the death squads of the Nazi war machine.

In 1944 her entire family was arrested by Nazi SS troops. All her family died during the Holocaust. Corrie survived the Concentration Camps after suffering great hardships and grueling humiliations at the hands of the Nazis. After the war she wrote a book, The Hiding Place, documenting her horrific ordeal with the Nazis during W.W. II.

During my time with Corrie, it became very evident that she did not have an once of resentment towards Germany. Corrie simply loved the German people. When asked why or how she could actually love the very people that killed her family. Her response was simple and pure, "Because my Heavenly Father forgives and loves them."

When I returned to Lausanne after the Olympics were concluded, I got together with Loren Cunningham and prayed, asking our Beloved Father what my next step should be. We waited on the Holy Spirit, believing that guidance would be revealed to me.

The Voice spoke these three simple words into my thoughts: "Go home now."

Just those simple three words would change my life forever.

Break on Through to the Other Side

Marty filming at the 1972 Munich Olympics

Story 28:
Hello America, I'm Back

*The manner of those who have learned to hear
the voice of the Voice have devoted much time alone
with the beloved and listening with an open heart—
a lot of listening.*
—Uncle Bear

I gave my VW bus to a friend who needed it. The cheapest flight I could find to get back to California was out of Frankfurt, Germany. I took a train from Lausanne, and by the time we reached Frankfurt, it was late at night. The youth hostel had locked its doors for the night. I really did not want to pay for an expensive hotel room.

I prayed and asked my Beloved One what I should do. "Sisters of Mary," popped into my thoughts, and I said, "*Yes!*"

I had visited them a few months previously, on a YWAM field trip. Those dear sisters were the closest I could have ever imagined to what angels would be like. They were such a trip, and I loved them.

I was fortunate to catch the last bus of the day to Darmstadt from Frankfurt. It was nearly midnight when I arrived at the Darmstadt bus station. I walked about a mile to the front gate of the Evangelical Sisterhood of Mary, led by Mother Basilea Schlink. They had built their monastery brick by brick from the ruins of the devastation of Darmstadt during WWII.

I meekly pressed on the doorbell. No one came for what felt like ages. I was now embarrassed, but didn't know what else to do. It was late at night, and I had nowhere to spend the night. I rang the bell again and prayed.

This time a dear sister did open the front door, and made her way to the gate. She didn't look all that happy to see me.

She asked, "What can I do for you at this hour of the night?"

"Do you happen to have a place where I could sleep for the night?"

She said, "I will be back, wait here."

I stood there in the dark cold of the night, and wondered if I should walk back to the bus station to sleep on a bench.

I thought, *Yeah, I'd better go.*

I turned around and started to walk away, very discouraged.

To my utter surprise, I heard a lovely, upbeat voice calling to me in an almost singsong rhythm of delight. I turned to see who was calling to me, and there were three sisters standing in the doorway, each holding a candle. They had really big smiles and joyful countenances. I was embarrassed and very tired—holding back tears of relief. It was dark outside, but it seemed to me as if each face had a warm, heavenly glow.

"Your room is ready, please come in and find rest," chimed one of the sisters.

I followed their lead. They giggled all the way down the hallway leading to my room. A big, old wooden door was opened in front of me.

One of the other dear sisters said, "This is your own room."

She said it in such a loving way that it really did feel like my room.

I slowly entered. It was candlelit, with a big basket of food on the table, and a little pot of hot tea.

The third sister spoke-up, "Have a wonderful time of rest."

Then all three sisters in a delightful harmonious singsong tone chimed, "Our dear brother, it is an great honor to have you with us." I truly felt like royalty.

As I entered the room, I thanked them for their hospitality and kindness. They giggled with delight as they bid me good night and slowly

Story 28: Hello America, I'm Back

closed the huge wooden door. I felt the presence of the Presence powerfully in the room and I thought, *This is surely a thin place.*

I wondered—*Had I just been welcomed by three angelic hosts?* I slept like a man without a care in the world. It seemed to me that Jesus had indeed prepared a place for me. My faith was encouraged for what awaited me in the United States.

When I boarded the jetliner in Frankfurt the next day, bound for New York City, my confidence in the Eternal One had been renewed. Time seemed to fly by on that trip across the Atlantic. At the New York airport, everyone looked to be in a big hurry to pass through customs.

I, on the other hand, was in no hurry to face the customs officer. I stood in the longest line, silently praying like a monk on a day pass. I waited patiently for my turn to present my passport to the customs officer. Finally, it was my turn.

The customs officer eyed me with a look that could air-condition an auditorium. He turned to his left and opened an enormous book of records and warrants to see if my name was in it. This was before the days of computer ID checking. I knew my name would be in the book. A friend had told me that he had seen my picture on the wall of a post office. He thought I was on the top ten most wanted list.

But I trusted the words, "Go home now." I believed the voice of the Voice had spoken to me. The officer looked up at me again—staring into my eyes as if he were in a trance or something. He then closed the enormous book, stamped my passport, and said, "Welcome home."

I smiled and said, "*Yes, sir, I'm going home.*"

I could not wipe the smile from my face before my flight to Los Angeles. I knew that God was with me—and that everything was going to be all right. The fear of my impending day in court, and what the judge might do to me, had been completely lifted temporarily from my shoulders.

I had an emotional reunion with my parents back in Anaheim. It was getting late and I was really tired from such a long and emotional day, so I said my good nights, kissed my mom, and headed for the bedroom. I was back in the bed that I had slept in for the better part of my first eighteen years.

I had pulled the drapes back and opened the window, in hopes that the fragrance of the night blooming jasmine outside my window would bless me with its intoxicating presence. To my surprise and delight, not only did I have the good fortune of the aroma of the jasmine; it was a full moon. It was so big and white, I wondered if I was seeing the famous blue moon? It was intensely brilliant, and there appeared to be a blue hue encircling its perimeter.

My thoughts drifted to Mindy. I knew she was only a thousand miles to the north of me. She felt much closer to me than the miles that separated us. I deeply missed her. My heart ached for her, and within a few minutes, romantic thoughts poured into my mind.

My old desk was still in its same location against the wall, next to my bed. I opened the top drawer, looking for a pen and paper. They were there, waiting for me to give them life. I quickly put words to the thoughts that captivated my emotions.

My White Rose Moon
Gently, within your ring of blue
Soft green eyes, my view in you
I beheld, the sacred pools of Hana
Floating free, bathed in beauty, Selah.

Behold, you are fair my love
Your long blond hair waves free in the breeze
Woven, silk soft, my fond dove
Radiant moonshine, always at ease.

My White Rose Moon,
I sought for you, in the night
Only to touch you from my dreams
You are softly, my delight
Our faces warmed by moonbeams.

Story 28: Hello America, I'm Back

The next morning I added a few details of my flight home and of some current affairs on a separate piece of paper, and folded them together before I licked the envelope and sealed it with a kiss.

The happy reunion with my parents didn't last very long. It was time for me to set up my day in court, which would also be the day I turned myself in to the law authorities of the state of Iowa.

I got a haircut and shaved off my beard. I even borrowed a sport coat and tie for the big day. I cleaned up pretty good. On the day of my court appearance, I showed up fifteen minutes early, walked up to the court bailiff, and said, "*Hi, I'm Martin Berry, and I'm here for my day in court.*"

He pointed to the left side of the courtroom and said, "Sit over there in one of the front two rows." I didn't know it at the time, but the bailiff mistakenly thought I was Martin Berry's legal representative.

I casually walked to the front row and sat down. A few minutes later, a door opened on the far right side of the courtroom, and in came four men, all dressed in faded blue, long-sleeved shirts and blue jeans. They were all handcuffed and chained together by ankle locks.

I thought, *Wow, do they look like criminals.*

I giggled to myself and thought, *I sure am glad I'm not chained up to those guys.*

The judge had their handcuffs and ankle locks removed. Then he went through each of their cases with amazing speed, and for the most part treated each one mercifully.

The plaintiff just before my turn with the judge was a repeat offender. The judge greeted him like they were old friends.

"Well, let's see why you are before me this time. It looks like you tried to hold up the same gas station again."

"Yes sir, that's exactly what I did, and I'm really sorry that I went and done such a stupid thing again."

"It says here on the affidavit that the service station has since been closed, out of business. Is that true to the best of your knowledge?"

"Yes sir, I do believe they've shut 'er down fer good."

"Well, I guess that means you won't be trying to hold it up again in the future."

"Yes sir, that is the truth. I will not be trying to hold up that there gas station ever again."

"Case dismissed!"

Case dismissed? I could not believe my own ears. The judge just cut loose a repeat offender. I was delighted with this judge. He seemed to be in a very good mood, and was being extremely lenient.

I thought, *This guy is the perfect judge for my hearing.*

It was finally my turn. The bailiff called out, "Martin Berry versus the state of Iowa."

I stood up, and the judge did a double take, looking from one side of the courtroom to the other. He appeared startled, and the pleasant expression on his face changed to one of sternness and a frown.

I had paid a Davenport, Iowa lawyer to set up my day in court. But I didn't see any reason to pay him to represent me at the actual hearing, in that I was pleading guilty as charged. The bailiff had mistakenly directed me to sit with the other lawyers, not fully understanding that I was Martin Berry, and I was there to turn myself in to the authorities.

Two policemen rushed over to me, grabbed me on either side, and said, "You are under arrest!"

I did not know what was going on. After all, I was there to turn myself in. They promptly marched me to the other side of the courtroom with the other criminals. The judge read the charges against me, and then made some remarks about how many people had written letters on my behalf.

"I have in front of me a number impressive letters from what appears to be some important people in Europe and the United States. They seem to claim that you, Martin Berry, have given your life to God, and consequently have been rehabilitated."

"*Yes, sir, that would be correct. I've given my life to Jesus Christ, and I have been rehabilitated by the grace of God.*"

Story 28: Hello America, I'm Back

"Well, young man, I am perplexed by all of this." He continued, "Martin Berry how do you plead to all of these charges?"

"*Guilty, sir. I am guilty as charged regarding the armed robbery and fleeing the country, but I never did anything to try to overthrow the United States government.*"

The judge paused and said, "I see here that you have never been arrested for any other crime."

"*That is true, Your Honor.*"

"Why should you not pay the penalty for your crimes?" the judge asked.

"*Well, sir, that is a really good question, and my only answer is that Jesus Christ has forgiven me, and the Spirit of God has changed my life.*"

"So, Christ Almighty has forgiven you, and God has changed you from a criminal to a law-abiding citizen, and that is your defense?"

"*Yes, sir, that is my only defense.*"

He paused again and looked up to the ceiling. I hoped he was thinking about God Almighty, and how forgiveness could actually change a life.

After the long pause, he picked up his gavel and said in a loud voice, "We will let the state of Iowa decide whether or not you have been rehabilitated. I sentence you to a ten-year prison term, to take effect immediately at the Iowa State Penitentiary at Anamosa."

Then he slammed his gavel down and said in a loud voice, "Court dismissed!"

Story 29:
Anamosa State Penitentiary

*Unbelief is faith on a weekend pass, but unfortunately,
Sometimes, it turns into a lifelong vacation.*
—Uncle Bear

I was immediately taken from the courtroom to the county jail, in a van with the other prisoners. I was now one of them, a criminal, a convict. I was on the verge of crying, but I reminded myself that weakness of this sort could encourage abuse and who knows what else from the other convicts. So I held back the tears, and just stared out the window of the van as we made our way to the county jail.

The next day, I was rudely awakened by a mean-looking guard.

"Get up Berry, your bus is waiting for you. Put on your shoes, let's get moving." It was 6:00 a.m. when he unlocked my jail door and ordered me to get moving.

I sheepishly asked, *"Do I get breakfast or coffee before we go?"*

He was not amused, or concerned in the least about my need for nourishment.

He barked at me, "Shut up! This is not a hotel, you damn idiot."

To say I was discouraged does not even come close to how low and defeated I felt that day. Twelve of us were loaded into the dreary state penitentiary bus that morning. There were bars on the windows and two armed guards.

Story 29: Anamosa State Penitentiary

I began to think about all the freedoms I had lost in less time than, one day. I could not go anywhere I wanted to go. I could not take a leisurely walk in the park or around the block. The simple freedoms and pleasures of life that I had taken for granted were now gone—long gone. I thought about Mindy and how much I missed her. I could see her lovely face in my mind's eye.

I had no idea what a ten-year sentence meant in real years. I knew some people had gotten out of prison early for good behavior.

I thought, *Gee, maybe with good behavior, I could get my sentence cut in half to five years.*

I think I would have thrown up right then and there if I had eaten any breakfast.

I had never known what a bottomless hole of despair could feel like, and despair is not the kind of dungeon you want to hang out in for very long. My mind began to wander down the lonely path of depression.

When I get out of prison, everything will have changed. Mindy won't wait for me, and how could I even expect her to wait for me? She is a teenager!

During that bus ride to the Anamosa State Penitentiary, I quickly came to the conclusion that I might have completely ruined my life and my future. I was on the verge of screaming out loud when I heard the words, "Open the gate!" The state trooper bus driver made the demand over what looked to be a CB shortwave radio. "Open the gate, we are approaching the entrance."

I strained to look ahead to see the old walls of the Anamosa prison. There it was: walls of solid rock and cement that must have reached seventy-five feet into the air.

The first feature that grabbed my attention was a guard tower looming over the entry gate. I could see a guard carrying what looked like a machine gun. Later, I discovered that each corner of the prison's outer wall had a guard tower. Each tower had a guard present twenty-four hours a day, with a machine gun, a shotgun, and a .352 side arm at his disposal.

Break on Through to the Other Side

The massive gate swung open, and the bus crept forward until we were inside the prison gate. As soon as we were clear of the entry wall, the gate closed behind us. All of a sudden, I was experiencing a very weird feeling, and a thought popped into my head, *You will not leave here alive.*

A chill ran through my body, and the hair on my arms literally stood up on end as my skin tightened with the thought of death. *I might not leave this place alive.* Well, if ever I thought a demon had just popped a thought into my brain, it was then.

I just kept repeating to myself, *Perfect love casts out all fear. Perfect love casts out all fear.* I repeated those words continuously my first day in prison.

The driver turned the bus sharply to the left after clearing the gated wall, then drove it onto the grass of the prison yard, and stopped in front of an old building with the words Receiving & Discharge written over its two huge doors.

My attention drifted toward some wonderful memories of being with Mindy in Switzerland. We took a lot of long walks through alpine meadows. Several times, we would take a picnic lunch with us. She loved picking wildflowers. Wow, did I ever miss her!

"You will never see her again," whispered a voice of darkness in my thoughts. I reacted with a surge of anger.

Damn it, demon! You are really getting on my nerves. If you don't back off, I'm going to cast you into the prison septic tank where you belong. This little mind game I was playing with a demon was all done silently. I had not spoken a word out loud.

A guard with a sawed-off shotgun walked up to me on the bus, got right in my face, and said, "Something bothering you inmate Berry?" And then he grinned at me with the weirdest, twisted expression on his face.

He yelled, "All right, ladies, this is our last stop of the day. It's time to get off the bus. Remember, do not make any sudden movements, and walk in single file into the Receiving & Discharge building." Meanwhile,

Story 29: Anamosa State Penitentiary

a large number of inmates had walked in our direction from the open prison yard.

Anamosa State Penitentiary

Story 30:
The Yard

Being controlled by something larger, older, greater, and more powerful than ourselves can be humiliating. However, it can be accepted as a relief, and a kind of letting go of our illusions of grandeur. Humiliation can be converted into humility and honor, if we embrace it.
—Uncle Bear

The yard was where the inmates could get outside for exercise, lifting weights, shooting hoops, smoking cigarettes, making contacts, buying drugs, hanging out with their respective gangs, and so on.

The twelve of us from the bus lined up single file, and started to walk toward the R&D building. Several inmates yelled catcalls at us.

"Hey, sweet thing, I'll be your daddy."

"Look at the fresh meat, I can't wait to get some of that fresh tender stuff."

"Welcome to camp hell, baby cakes."

"Join a gang, or plan on getting gang-banged."

Fear was not my friend—nor was fear a good counselor—but nevertheless, fear had made its way into my head. I knew it was the power of darkness at work, but it got into my mind anyway. I felt embarrassed, and a bit ashamed that the pendulum of my emotions had swung so quickly from trust in the I Am to a pathetic, worrisome fright.

Story 30: The Yard

I was relieved when we were finally inside the R&D building, but that relief didn't last long. A guard inside the building shouted commands at us. "All right, jail birds, strip 'em off." He held up an empty metal basket and said, "Take off all your clothes, and put all your belongings into one of these baskets. If and when you leave here, you will get them back, or we will send them to your nearest relative."

After we had removed our clothing, watches, rings, and anything else we might have had on us, they took us one at a time into a room. There we were searched for hidden drugs and the like. Then we were led into another room, where the job of that attending officer was to dump lice powder from head to toe on each of us. Finally, we were led to a shower room, where we could wash off the lice powder.

As we left the shower room, we were provided a towel for drying off, after which we were to throw the towel into a huge laundry basket. Stripped naked, searched, deloused, washed and dried—I had never experienced such humiliation. Naked, we moved on in single file to our next stop, men's apparel.

The inmate supervisor of the garment habitat looked us up and down while we stood there in our birthday suits. He then yelled out sizes. "Give me two large work shirts, two large white T-shirts, two pairs of pants thirty-four by thirty-two, and two pairs of large briefs." He was pretty good at his occupation. He nailed my sizes right down to the size ten work shoes. For the final touch, the apparel apprentice would stamp each man's convict number across the front of his two faded blue work shirts. It was now official—I was 203103.

Then I was singled out, for no apparent reason, "Inmate Berry, you follow me."

I asked him politely, "*Where are you taking me?*"

"Oh, I'm taking you to a special place where we take the new convicts who have a crime of violence on their sentencing sheet." He laughed and then continued, "I'm taking you to the hole—you know, the dungeon."

We walked down three very long hallways, and then down a couple of flights of stairs. Wherever we were headed, those stairs smelled dank, dirty, and exceedingly moldy. It took a few minutes for my eyes to adjust to the lack of light. The guard unlocked a cell and said, "Welcome to your new home for the next twenty-one days."

I could hardly believe what he had just said. "Your new home for the next twenty-one days!"

"Three weeks—dang, that's a long time to be in solitary confinement."

"Now you are getting it. The twenty-one days are designed to let you know up front who the boss is at Anamosa."

I tried to adjust to my surroundings. My cell was approximately five feet wide and eight feet long. The forty-square-foot suite would be my new digs. It had a solid metal bed two feet wide that was permanently welded to the wall, with a two-inch-thick, hard, old pad on it. There were two sheets and one blanket folded at the foot of the bed, with a pillow on top. At the opposite end of the cell was an aluminum one-piece toilet/sink combination.

I decided to make my bed. When I picked up the pillow, to my surprise, a tiny pencil and a small note pad greeted me. I thought it odd that a guard would leave me such a gift. Then it occurred to me that maybe they had to give you some vehicle to communicate with the world outside these walls—even if you were in the dungeon for three weeks.

I must admit, my first day and night in solitary confinement was pretty depressing. I felt abandoned, and thought I had completely ruined my life at the ripe old age of twenty-three. I didn't sleep much that first night in the dungeon. I mainly felt confused, hopeless, and forgotten. My attitude toward my Heavenly Father was not exactly pleasant that night.

Finally, after several hours, my utterly boring self-pity party was over. I comforted myself in the middle of the night with thoughts and memories of Mindy. Only weeks ago, Mindy and I had walked hand in hand down the cobblestone streets of Lausanne and had walked in a boundless green valley with the Alps towering above us. Oh, I so enjoyed our walks together.

Story 30: The Yard

Mindy simply and genuinely loved people. She had a delightful gift of connecting her heart and emotions into action whenever the need arose. I had never met or been with anyone who was so naturally alive and lovely. She celebrated life in the moment. Her love for people was contagious. I could see it in the faces of people who merely made eye contact with her as we passed them on the street. They would smile spontaneously, as if by some spiritual osmosis. A spark of life, an elusive, subtle, warm glow would ever so slightly enhance their countenance.

I, on the other hand, had the perspective of celebrating life in the future, after I had accomplished some extraordinary endeavor or feat. The future never met me in the now. It was always just ahead of me, and I was reaching for it. I guess this would explain some of the continual emotional frustration that hounded me before the presence of the Presence became known to me.

The thought occurred to me that she very well could be the first absolutely wonderful person I had ever met, and she loved me. She loved me!

I did not feel worthy of such love. This tunnel of thought led me into a dark downward spiral of free-falling false humility. Before I could stop the gravity of the whirling force of my emotions of doubt and despair, I had convinced myself that it would be completely unfair of me to expect Mindy to wait for me. After all, I had just begun to serve a ten-year sentence at the Anamosa State Penitentiary in Iowa. She had only turned seventeen a few weeks earlier. Mindy would still be a teenager for nearly three more years.

The morning after my first day in solitary confinement, I wrote Mindy a letter that I would deeply regret in the weeks to follow. I told her that we should just be friends, and that she should be open to whomever God might bring into her life.

The remainder of the day was spent in remorse over what a complete disaster I had made of my life. It felt like something of myself was dying. The hours passed with much groaning and weeping, until I fell into a deep sleep.

Story 31:
Marty the Monk

Thank you prison, thank you solitary confinement,
bless you for being in my life.
For there, alone in the darkness,
I came to realize that the purpose of my life
was not prosperity, position, or power.
—Uncle Bear

The sun did rise the next morning, just as it had for the past twenty-two years of my life. But something was different. I had changed. I was no longer a happy-go-lucky youth, with years of good times and carefree fun in the sun ahead of me. I had changed.

I felt old. I was used up and had nowhere to go—but I was totally, absolutely, completely in the here and now. I wasn't going anywhere. I was in solitary confinement for the next three weeks. I thought, *What in the world am I going to do?*

Beloved Father, please help me, I don't know what to do. I am so lost, and I can't go anywhere. I don't know what to do or say. I need help! Dear Holy One, please help me. I went silent, and started to weep quietly.

I don't know how long I sat in silence, weeping before the I Am. It could have been minutes or hours. Time seemed to stand still or not exist at all. I was in a very strange place of the unknown and the not-yet. I fell asleep—for how long I don't know. The space-time continuum had ended for me.

Story 31: Marty the Monk

Upon awakening, I felt kind of odd. Something had happened inside of me, in my soul or my spirit, or maybe both. I felt strangely encouraged. Somehow, I knew the Holy One had gifted me with something. I no longer felt alone or fearful. With inward contemplation, I could sense something new inside me. It was like a fast reserve, a deep reservoir of peace and silent strength within me. I possessed courage.

I now knew what it was like to have a metaphor become real. Living water was in my belly and flowing. I had never experienced anything like that before. I knew in my knower that the Eternal One had a purpose for me in this prison—and the dungeon of solitary confinement was my training camp. I needed time alone with the I Am.

I was to become *Marty the Monk!* Pure and simple, I was to receive a symbolic, metaphoric monk's robe. I sat in glorious silence for untold hours. The presence of the Presence was thick. I was in a thin place, as the ancient Celts used to call it; a place where the Presence is very near and dear.

My communion with the One, my Eternal Father, the Christ Spirit, and the wondrous, ever-present Holy Spirit was extraordinary and dazzling. They, the Three in One, were swirling around me in my little universe, my cell. It was a baptism in the Presence.

I sat in silence for God only knows how long. After the stillness of being thoroughly occupied by the fullness of the void, words began to form without any effort or thought. At first I didn't know if the words were silent or aloud. Finally, the words became apparent to me. Softly at first, but after not too long a time, the words began to get louder and louder with enthusiasm and vitality. The volume and breadth of my prayers were rising with the tide of the overwhelming presence of the Voice, the Word, the Truth.

It wasn't very long thereafter that I began to sing spontaneously, like an Irish tenor late on a Friday night at the pub. I sang, and I sang, and I sang! Then, out of the vacuum of the dungeon, came a screeching guttural voice of disapproval. The voice did not sound human.

It really hadn't occurred to me that others would be down here in this dark, dingy place.

I thought, *How odd of me to think that I would be the only one in solitary confinement.* I guess I was in such a state of shock when they brought me in that it just hadn't entered my mind.

The demented, tortured voice continued with much cursing and many obscenities not worth repeating to anyone. Others joined in on the trash-talking melee of insults and threats.

I soon learned that more than just a few others were locked up in the dungeon with me. Many seemed to favor the dark shadows of lostness. It seemed that the dye had been cast. They had tired of my singing and lifting my voice in praise to the Holy One. They could no longer hold back the darkness that swelled from within their wounded, tormented souls.

For no obvious reason, they seemed to hate me. All, that is, except one poor soul. When all the cursing and yelling at me quieted down and silence became the norm, I could vaguely hear a whimpering sound from the cell next to me. I listened as intently as possible—and I was sure. The unknown, unseen person in the cell next to me was softly crying and moaning in grievous pain.

After much coaxing on my part, he responded to my attempts to communicate with him. In very soft tones, he said he had been in a fight. His forearm just above the wrist had been smashed and broken by a cast-iron pipe. He was in agonizing pain, because the doctors would not prescribe anything for the pain. He was in prison for selling heroin, and was an addict himself; therefore, he could not have any pain-killers.

I asked him if I could pray for him, but he preferred being left alone. I think he didn't want anyone to know that he could possibly be my friend.

I didn't understand why I was experiencing such rejection and ill will from my fellow inmates. However, it would not be long before I would find out why they hated me so much.

Story 31: Marty the Monk

I knew it must be lunchtime, because a tin platter was pushed through the tiny little door. The little door resembled something I had once seen at a friend's house. Their cat could come and go as it pleased through a tiny swinging gate in a door, but the tiny door here slid sideways by the hand of the guard. I felt like Alice in Wonderland, and I was waiting to become ten feet tall.

I called out to the guard, "*Officer! Officer! I need to ask you a question.*"

He barked back at me, "Inmate Berry, what do you want?"

"*Sir, I would really appreciate having a Bible in here.*"

He didn't answer me, but at suppertime, when he pushed my tin plate through the tiny door, it was accompanied by an old, dilapidated Bible.

I yelled, "*Thank you, sir!*"

He did not answer me back.

During daylight hours, when they left the lights on, I could barely make out the words on the pages, but I was still very grateful. I read it for hours on end, until my eyes were so tired that I could no longer focus on the words.

An inconvenience is only an adventure wrongly considered.
—G. K. Chesterton

Story 32: War in the Dungeon

*Knowing the difference between your survival dance
and embracing your sacred dance is the essential requisite
for the Big Dance that awaits us.*
—Uncle Bear

As Marty the Monk, knowing that you are what you seek became a game changer for me. Thereby, I developed some new habits. A priceless gift was emerging within me. I was beginning to be able to stop the endless chatter of my own mind, my ego-driven false self. I was learning to let the new man—the true self—bask in the countenance of the Christ Spirit. To sit in silence and be still, knowing the I Am is with me. Space and time lost its importance, but the presence of the Presence meant everything.

I pondered at length many New Testament scriptures of the Bible for hours on end each day. I often read it out loud for thespian effect, and so that I could hear the words as well as read them. I would meditate on the words of scripture I had read, and practice being silent in the presence of the Presence. My old thoughts and made to order interpretations of days gone by made way for the Way. To my delight, many versus began to take on new, expanded, metaphoric meaning.

My prayers had become totally relational. I very seldom asked for anything. I couldn't help but laugh at my old shopping list style of previous prayer. I just liked hanging out with the Beloved. I had a profound awareness that the Eternal One was in the cell with me. Most of the time,

Story 32: War in the Dungeon

I prayed out loud in a soft voice. When I prayed silently, it usually turned out to be more contemplative and curious. I thought a lot about the mysteries of Christ and His created universe.

After the first week, I actually began to enjoy the solitary confinement lifestyle. In the physical, I was most certainly held captive—but in my soul and spirit, I was experiencing such wonderful peace and freedom. Freedom I had never known before.

I had become very aware that the distractions of everyday life could be, and many times are, deadly for our true self. For the first time in my life, I could see the difference between my false self and my new true self. I pondered the possibility that Lucifer, the devil himself, could actually be working behind the scenes of many modern-day conveniences, to keep us preoccupied and distracted from finding and being alone in the presence of the Presence.

It became clear to me that much—no, most—of my life was self-centered and all about my ego gratification. My self-image was not built around the image of the Holy Spirit in me. Most of my self-image was built around *me, me, me, and I, I, I*. The Holy One was graciously making me aware of how selfish and self-centered I had been for the greater part of my life.

In my Christian walk, I had asked for forgiveness many times before, mainly out of guilt or shame, but my life hadn't seemed to change much. True change began to come with the awareness that I was, plain and simple, a sinner. Yes, I had committed a myriad of actual sins, but that wasn't the main game anymore. The guilt and shame game had been exposed for what it was, and I was being freed from it.

Now it was as if layers of selfishness, guilt, and shame were being lifted off me. The awareness of my selfish, self-centered preoccupation with me, and what I wanted for food, drink, entertainment, and a myriad of other false comforts, was being brought into the light of the Light. God so graciously brought these awakenings to my conscious awareness during those soul-searching hours alone with my Spirit Father.

It became very clear to me that salvation was not a one-time decision or experience, but much more like a doorway that opens to an eternal adventure with and into Oneness. My life was to be in Christ, not about Christ. It was during these priceless weeks of solitary confinement that I first began to see clearly the immense difference between a "human doing" and a "human being."

Jesus once said, "The truth shall set you free." I think Jesus could have extended the saying with these words, *The Truth will make you miserable for a while, but it will in due time set you free.* I was suffering a little in my flesh, but the suffering was sweet. There was no longer a laundry list of sins I had committed. I was being set free from myself, and my endless ego gratification.

I learned by revelation and experience that Jesus the Christ was and is the Truth, the Way, and the Light. Christ and I spent many hours of every day in the dungeon together. I believe I was experiencing something akin to a genuine transformation from my old, shadow self into my new, true self. The constant chatter of useless thoughts was subsiding. I became aware that many, if not most, people have a very difficult time hearing the inward voice of God, because their own voice is so loud.

I had never experienced such freedom and joy before in my entire life. Salvation, redemption, sin, forgiveness, glory, worship, holiness, and grace all became more than just religious words found in the Bible. They became living words, with their own life and energy within me. Old things were passing away, and I was becoming new, newer, and renewed.

Now I understood why the mystic Christian monks of centuries past would delight in their hermitages as places to be alone with the Eternal One. Of course, with all this spiritual stuff happening to me while in solitary confinement, I did wonder from time to time if, in this modern world of constant distractions and ego stimulus, there was a way for anyone to have this experience of really being alone with the One.

One day, while having a wonderful time reading the Bible out loud and speaking of the wonders of the I Am, I began to sing in the Spirit's gift of my spirit language—just as the early disciples did when the Holy Spirit came upon them on the first celebration of Pentecost after the resurrection of Christ Jesus.

It was glorious. I sang and sang to my heart's delight. Unfortunately, it didn't last long enough. I could hear the dark voices again screaming

Story 32: War in the Dungeon

profanities at me. But this time, by a spontaneous response of power and authority within me, I could hear myself rebuking the devil.

Other inmates in the dungeon joined in on what seemed to be a cursing match. It was as if each voice was trying to outdo the other in how profane and disgusting its tirade of insults, threats, and obscene accusations could possibly be.

Boldness came upon me, like nothing I had ever experienced before. From the core of my soul came powerful rebukes, not at the inmates, but at the spirits that tormented them. I was fully engaged in spiritual war in the dungeon. I could not see any of the poor souls who were possessed or plagued by darkness. I could only hear them for the time being.

The barrage of disgusting filth continued to spew from their human lips. However, the Spirit was heavily upon me. One by one, the demons were silenced. Some demons came out through loud screaming, others through coughing, and a few through loud weeping. When all was said and done, the demons had retreated to a hiding place of dark despair and resignation.

The Prince of Peace now ruled in the dungeon. I had discovered through the experience of this battle something hidden, and yet obvious. The authority that was and is in His name is in us, if we are in Christ—not by mere association with His name, but only by an actual ongoing spiritual experience of practicing the presence of the One.

I now knew that being a Christian in name only was like looking in the mirror and believing your reflected image is the real you—when in truth, it is only a superficial impression of our outer layer. Hidden within each of us is an eternity of value that is unsurpassable. It does give cause to wonder why so much attention and image worship is given to the outer layer, which will sooner or later pass away.

> *In the end, we will remember not the words of our enemies,*
> *but the silence of our friends.*
> —Martin Luther King Jr.

Story 33: Welcome to the Neighborhood

*Essentially nothing would be accomplished,
if we waited until there was no risk, flaw, or fear.
Opportunity might not be knocking,
but she will dance with those who have the courage
to get on the dance floor.*
—Uncle Bear

My three weeks in isolation, which I lovingly called the dungeon, seemed to fly by quickly. The other unseen inmates in solitary confinement had become somewhat friendly toward me. Well, at least they stopped yelling profanities at me, and for the most part were fairly quiet.

On the morning of my twenty-second day, I was escorted to my cellblock by one of the guards. When we arrived, he asked me what floor I wanted to be on. I chose the sixth floor, because it was as high as you could go. It was the top floor, and I knew I needed all the exercise I could get in here.

The guard and I climbed the six flights of stairs, then he opened one of the empty cells and said, "Don't make any enemies up here. They have been known to throw people who didn't belong here over the railing."

I was a little confused, so I asked the guard, *"What is that supposed to mean, not belong here?"*

Story 33: Welcome to the Neighborhood

"This is the penthouse—most everyone up here are lifers. Generally speaking, you need to either earn your way, or be invited to the penthouse."

"Why didn't you tell me that before you gave me this cell?"

He grinned and said, "You are not my problem or my responsibility, and besides that, things have been a little boring around here lately."

Within a few minutes, three Latino permanent residents of the penthouse came up to me and asked, "Who do you think you are, moving into our hood?"

"You got a death wish or something?"

"No! Well actually, I do in a way. I want to give my life and spend eternity with the Holy One."

They just stared at me with bewildered expressions, until one of them spoke, "Loco, man. I'm telling you this dude is loco."

"OK, let me try to explain. The Christ said if you lose your life for my sake, you will actually receive life—eternal life."

"Whoa! Dude, you really are completely loco."

"You think you belong up here with us because you are crazy, and we are supposed to be cool with that?"

Ah, yes. I had hoped you would welcome me to your neighborhood.

"Hippie, what is your name?"

"Marty Berry was my name the last time I checked. But you can call me Marty, Marty the Monk, if you want."

They looked at each other with confused expressions. The one who had not said a word pulled at his goatee. It was as if he was contemplating something really heavy.

Finally he spoke, "Loco, completely loco. And I'm OK with that. Here's where it's at—I say we let him stay in the penthouse."

The other two nodded their heads in agreement.

I smiled and simply said, *"Far-out!"*

"It is great to be a part of your neighborhood."

I extended by hand to shack theirs, as a sign of friendship.

But my offer was met with these words, "Don't press your luck hippie."

"*Yeah OK! I'm cool with that.*"

I knew that God had given me favor with these guys. They could have started off my first day in the general prison population in a very bad way. I really did want to see Jesus—I just didn't really want to see him right then.

I was allowed to send out mail while in solitary, but I had not received any. Now I knew why. A bundle of letters was brought to my new residence on the sixth floor. I quickly thumbed through them to see who had written me. There it was, the letter I most wanted to see, a letter from Mindy.

I quickly opened it, but to my disappointment these words jumped off the page, "Your letter broke my heart, but I will try to understand. Yes, I will be your friend."

I thought, *Marty, what have you done. Why did you tell her it would be best if we were just friends? What have you done, you dumb ass?*

I was trying to act spiritual without being spiritual. I was trying to do the right thing without being right. I learned a very hard lesson that day. That *good intentions* sometimes pave the way for disappointment and despair, unless they are inspired by the Holy One.

It was high noon, twelve o'clock, and everyone knew what that meant: time to eat lunch in the huge cafeteria. I was taken aback by its massive size. It was one enormous room, with the ceiling reaching at least forty or fifty feet above us. About halfway up the wall was a gangway that connected all four corners of the room. Guards walked the gangway, watching over us during every meal.

My first day in the yard was very interesting. I really didn't know anyone except the three guys I had met in the penthouse earlier that day. So I just kind of walked around, trying to get a feel for the place and the general population of the prison. Inmates were all over the prison yard, doing all sorts of different things in various groups. I tried to stay incognito while I casually walked and prayed silently.

My thoughts continued to return to the words of Mindy in her letter to me. I felt a little neurotic. Simultaneously, I felt an empty ache in

Story 33: Welcome to the Neighborhood

the pit of my stomach. Yet, at the same time, I felt the voice of the Voice within me surging for expression. I was not confused. There was a calmness that I did not understand.

A hippie with really long red hair approached me and he said, "Hi, are you the religious guy they call the monk—who has just spent the last three weeks in solitary?"

"*Yep, that would be me.*"

"Most everyone in the yard has heard about you and what you were doing in lockup. There are a lot of people who have been waiting for you to get released into the population."

"*Cool! That sounds great.*"

"No, man, it's not cool. The people who are waiting to meet you want to mess with you. They basically think you are some flipped-out hippie who is on some kind of a fanatical religious trip. So I wanted to warn you, before you get hammered by some of these questionable characters."

"*Wow, thanks, man. I appreciate your advice and concern.*"

"You need to know a few things before I leave—and I'm sorry."

"*You're sorry? Why are you sorry?*"

"I'm sorry because this will be the first and last time I will be talking to you."

"*Why is that?*"

"You are too dangerous to be seen with, or become friends with. Here is the last thing I can do for you. See the group of guys hanging around the hoops?"

"*Yeah, I see them.*"

"Don't try to mingle with them. They will hurt you. See the group over there against the wall catching some rays?"

"*Yes, I can see them.*"

"Don't ever be caught alone with any of them. They will rape you and turn you into their bitch. Now, this is the most important info I can tell you. See the group lifting weights?"

"*Yes, I can see that they look like they do a lot of weight lifting.*"

Break on Through to the Other Side

"Whatever you do, do not approach them, and never get caught alone with any of them. They could kill you, or worse. You might wish you were dead."

"*Wow, man. Thank you so much for taking the time and the risk of giving me the lowdown on what is up with the yard population.*"

I extended my hand to shake his in appreciation.

He put his hands in his coat pockets and said, "That's cool, man," and walked away with his head lowered, looking only at the ground in front of him.

I said a silent prayer, took a deep breath, and headed directly for the gang hanging out by the weights.

Story 34:
Big Bad John

*Breakdowns, obstacles, and danger are the terrifying things
you will see when you take your eyes off the purpose of the race
and forget why you are on the road less traveled.*
—Uncle Bear

I prayed silently while I walked toward the gang in the weight lifting area. The grace of God was heavily upon me, and a boldness from within rushed to the surface. I was fearless. I felt powerful and thoroughly alive.

As I approached them, one by one they stopped what they were doing, and looked up to see who dared come onto their turf. I was greeted with many insults regarding my person. "Hey, honky, what you doin', fool? White boy, you have come to the wrong party. Are you lookin' to die today?"

"*No, actually, I prefer living today.*"

"Well, then, tell us what the hell you are doing in our hood."

I paused for a moment to gather my thoughts before I answered him.

"Speak up, white bread, you damn idiot! What the hell are you doin' here?" They were getting noticeably very agitated by my presence.

I did not know what to say. So, I just opened my mouth and trusted that God would give me the right words to speak.

"*Your Heavenly Father knows why you are here, and he loves you anyway.*"

"Tell us fool, why are we here?"

They were now all on their feet and beginning to surround me. "Well, are you gonna tell us why we are here, fool?"

"*Yes, I will tell you why you are here. You are here because you are dirty, rotten criminals.*" I could not believe my own ears. *Did I really just say that?* I was completely surprised when they roared with laughter at what I had just blurted out.

The biggest muscle-bound guy of the gang stood directly in front of me. He was still holding onto his dumbbells, which looked to be fifty pounds each. He got within a few inches of my face and said, "You know, prison is a very dangerous place, and accidents happen all the time in here. As a matter of fact, I once saw a chump's head get smashed in by one of these dumbbells. As a matter of fact, I was trying to show him how to lift weights, when I accidentally smashed in his head."

I meekly asked, "*Is that why you are still in here?*"

He laughed in my face and said, "Oh, hell no. I was already doing three consecutive life sentences. I will never get out of this place, and the way it looks, you probably won't get out of here alive, either."

"*Yah know, brother, if you make it a habit threatening to kill people, you probably have a few enemies around here who want to kill you.*"

"Brother! I'm not your damn brother. My name is John."

Another voice chimed in, "Big John. Big Bad John."

A third gang member spoke up, "He has killed three other fools with his bare hands. Walk lightly, white boy."

I felt the power of the Holy One rising from within me. "*I'm not your boy. I'm not white bread, or anything else you call me. I am a living, flesh and blood representative of the eternal I Am, because I am in Christ.*"

They howled with laughter. But Big John didn't even smile. His eyes bulged out and became bloodshot. He was filled with anger and hatred as he looked down on me. "Maybe I should just send your ass home to your daddy God today."

"*John, you can kill me today, and I know where I will be going. But where will you go if someone kills you today?*"

Story 34: Big Bad John

"I will go to hell with the rest of these bastards."

"John, it doesn't have to be that way. Jesus gave His life so that you can have life and follow Him forever. Your previous shit and sins are forgiven. Jesus is who He said He was. And whether you like it or not, you are my brother. You just don't know it yet."

He opened both his hands and dropped the heavy dumb bells from waist height to the concrete slab beneath us. The noise of the heavy metal crashing into solid concrete was a loud, clanging, abrasive, sound. I felt its vibration under my feet.

He reached out his enormous right hand and brushed it against my neck as he rested it on my shoulder. His bulging bloodshot eyes began to tear up, and he said in a low, gruff tone, "I know that you are right, but I never really believed that God would ever forgive me for all the terrible things I have done to people—men and women."

"If God could forgive Moses, King David, and Paul, who were all murderers, he will forgive you. It is a gift, and a gift must be received to be yours."

I took a really deep breath and asked, *"Do you want to reach out and grab the gift of life, eternal life?"*

"Yes, I want it."

"Do you want to know Jesus and follow Him?"

"Yes man, I do." John couldn't speak out-loud any longer, as tears began to pour down his face.

John was the first convert I embraced in prison. John was no longer Big Bad John. He was now simply Big John—my brother and personal bodyguard. Whenever I walked the prison's yard, John was there by my side to make sure that whomever I was talking with would politely listen to me.

I thought I would wait awhile before I got around to telling John that he shouldn't intimidate or threaten people on my behalf. John became my best friend in the prison.

There was a chapel in the prison, but no one was ever there, except a very small handful on Sunday mornings. The prison chaplain was a kind, humble man. He gave me full rule and reign of the chapel, to meet there as often as I liked.

Within a month, there was standing room only every night of the week. About a hundred men had decided to follow Jesus that first month. The chaplain gave me the Sunday morning service. By the third month, we had two Sunday morning services, and one on Sunday night.

I'm really not sure how many men gave their lives to Jesus in those first three months. Someone told me that possibly half the inmates had changed the direction of their lives to follow Jesus, and there were around five hundred men in the Anamosa prison.

First they ignore you, then they laugh at you,
then they fight you, then you win.
—Mahatma Gandhi

Story 35: Receiving & Discharge

*I have been amazed and dumbfounded at how many people
don't know where they are going,
and they don't seem to care
if they don't get there.*
—Uncle Bear

At the end of my first month in Anamosa prison, I was asked to show up at the Receiving & Discharge building first thing Monday morning. To my surprise, I was asked to head up the photography in the prison because of my experience in video and photography. Mainly, that meant taking mug shots in Receiving when a new inmate arrived.

I was very grateful to be given this highly sought-after position. I had my own little partitioned office space, a desk, and of course the photo set, with a dark room for processing the film. The darkroom was my favorite place in the prison. It had a workbench, a big fan, and continuous running water for the developing solution.

While I was developing film, the door would be shut and the do not disturb light switch turned on, which meant a red light bulb was lit on the outside entry wall of the darkroom. This indicated that no one was supposed to open the darkroom door.

When I was in the darkroom, I had a prime commodity, privacy! Basically, no one has privacy in a prison, unless you are in solitary confinement. The darkroom became my prayer retreat, with the sound of a trickling brook, the wind of a waterfall, and a bench to recline upon. I could pray, sing, laugh, and contemplate the greatness of the Eternal One, without interruption. The darkroom was my private space to be alone with the Presence.

When a new inmate was processed in Receiving during his first day at Anamosa. The inmate would be directed into my office, there was a stool for the new arrival to sit on with stage lights on either side. Usually, by the time the person had gone through the other dehumanizing, humiliating procedures at Receiving, he was feeling pretty despondent.

I would tell the new inmate to sit down on the stool, and I would hand him a four-by-twenty-four-inch placard that had his convict number scrawled across it. I then directed him to hold the placard with both hands, chest high. It was now time to turn on those very bright stage lights.

It was impossible to see me behind those lights. All the new inmate could make out was my voice. So, there he was sitting on the stool, holding a placard across his chest that identified him only as a series of numbers. I would let him sit there with those blinding lights for a couple of minutes while I asked the Holy One for wisdom.

From behind the lights in the darkness, he could only hear my voice. Many of the encounters went something like this: "*You have completely screwed up your life, and maybe your future. What are you going to do? There is only one way out of the mess you have gotten yourself into. Do you want to know how to correct the course and the direction you are currently headed?*"

"Yeah, man, what do you mean? What can I do?"

"*Do you really want to know?*"

"Yes! I really want to know."

"*Here's what you need to do. You need to give your life to Jesus and daily commit to following the Christ.*"

To my surprise, about half of those guys would say, "Yes, I want to give my life to Jesus." I would then invite them to the meeting we held in the chapel every night.

Story 35: Receiving & Discharge

Of course, the guys who did not want to give their lives to Jesus would most often find me in the yard a day or two later and threaten me with bodily harm. But that was no big thing—I was threatened by some inmate just about every day.

Everything was going exceedingly well, except my relationship with Mindy. I had to give my love for her to God every day. I missed her terribly. I reminded myself daily that she was in God's hands, and my job was to trust the Holy One with all my heart. It wasn't easy when I would lay awake late into the night, thinking about her.

Dear Betty, Mindy's mother, wrote me every week, sometimes twice a week. She would encourage me to trust our Heavenly Father regarding the future with Mindy. She would send me pictures of Mindy, and tell me how well she was doing. Betty continually gave me hope. She inspired me to believe in the future, and my future with Mindy.

I had never met anyone like Betty before in my life. She believed in me. When it made no sense in the world to believe in me. Her faith seemed to birth faith in me. She gave me hope and I loved her for it.

After just three months in Anamosa, I was called before the parole board. This usually never happens until after the first year. I sat down and smiled at the members of the board. One of them said, "Marty, we see that you are no criminal."

I impulsively interrupted her. *"Excuse me, ma'am. I'm sorry, and I mean no disrespect, but I am a criminal. But Jesus in me is no criminal."*

"We agree with you to a degree. We do not approve of your methods, but we really do like the results. We are aware that you have had a somewhat miraculous effect on some of the men who will spend the remainder of their days here at Anamosa prison without any hope of parole."

"Oh, you mean some of the guys like Big John, Hit Man, White Lightening and Tank, to name only a few."

The bald man on the parole board spoke up, "Big John and some others did kind of run this place till they got religion."

"Well, sir, that is not entirely correct. John did not get religion. He got Jesus."

One of the other board members interrupted me, "Mr. Berry, we are not here to argue with you. As has been said, we like what we have seen of the results on the lives of some of the more hardened inmates. Many of them now display attributes of kindness and respect for the guards and other inmates. Simply said, we have called you here today to offer you a promotion of sorts. This has never been done before, but we are confident that you will not let us down."

I could not believe my own ears. *A promotion! What in the world were they talking about?*

"Marty, it will be your choice, but we recommend that you serve the remainder of your sentence at the Iowa Medical and Classification Center in Iowa City. You will be an aide, working with psychiatrists, medical doctors, and nurses. You will wear the standard white shirt, pants, and the shoes of a hospital aide. You will wear a badge identifying you as Aide Berry. You will not be required to wear any numbers that would identify you as a convict.

"You will have living quarters at the facility, but you will have minimum outs that will allow you to go shopping in Iowa City once a week. However, if you are found to be breaking any rules of conduct or with any contraband, you will be immediately returned to Anamosa prison, where you will spend the remainder of your sentence, and I assure you it will be hard time."

I took a deep breath, trying to maintain my composure. I accepted their offer, knowing that it was due to the favor of the Holy One. After thanking them for their humbling kindness and for giving me such an opportunity, I returned to my post at Receiving & Discharge. I felt really good about the parole board meeting.

I had no idea that it was the calm before the storm.

Story 36:
Welcome to the Cuckoo's Nest

A stubborn, sanctimonious, pious, self-righteous person convinced against their will, is of the same opinion still.
—Uncle Bear

When I first entered the medical facility just outside Iowa City, in a little town called Oakdale, I viewed my promotion as a blessing. It was great to be treated once again as a normal human being. I was no longer called an inmate or convict. I was no longer referred too by a number.

I was now respectfully called Aide Berry. Everyday, as an aide, I was asked to assist a doctor, nurse, or therapist for designated group therapy sessions. Other than the therapy sessions, it was my job to oversee the patients in their daily activities.

Unfortunately, the blessing of my promotion didn't last very long. I discovered that even though all the doctors, nurses, and aides wore white. It was a covering for the veiled, dark secrets hidden beneath the sterile facade of their outer clothing. A famous doctor once said, "Show me a sane man, and I will cure him for you." Dr. Carl Jung

The realization of this ever-present darkness became obvious the day the head doctor ordered me, in writing, to not share my religious beliefs regarding Jesus Christ with anyone at the Oakdale medical facility. I now felt trapped—my freedom had been taken from me.

I actually wondered if I had made a terribly wrong choice in coming to the Oakdale facility. However, through much prayer, I took strength and peace that the Holy One had indeed sent me to this place. Nevertheless, I did deeply miss the wild and crazy days for Jesus I'd had in prison. Here, I was treated with respect, and I was expected to act with respect toward the institution I now represented, to the letter of the law.

I no longer had the day-to-day joy of seeing lives changed, like I continually experienced at the Anamosa prison. I was not comfortable in this environment. I was dealing with a new kind of confinement—I was being persecuted for my relationship with Christ.

I knew in my heart that my Heavenly Father had promoted me to this place, but I wasn't sure what that promotion meant. I quickly learned it didn't mean an easier lifestyle. Remaining true to Christ was going to be rough, and even dangerous at times. In fact, my faith would be tested in ways I had never imagined possible in America.

I soon learned that sometimes we must go down in order to rise up to a new level. I did have a new kind of integrity in the lifestyle here, but with it came the threat of a noose tied around my neck. If I screwed up, they would tighten the noose.

I was now being motivated by fear, not unfettered faith. Many times a day, I would repeat the words, *"Be anxious for nothing, but in everything by prayer and supplication with thanksgiving, let your requests be made known to God; and the peace of God, which surpasses all understanding, will guard your hearts and minds in Christ Jesus." (Phil. 4:6-8)*

I had never believed that your heart could actually ache from the absence of someone you loved. Now I knew it was more than just possible. I missed, and literally ached for Mindy everyday.

I received a very timely, needed letter from her. Her tone had changed, and I sensed a renewed softness in her words. To my surprise and enormous satisfaction, Mindy announced that she was returning to Lausanne, Switzerland to attend the same YWAM school I had attended exactly one year earlier. This was great news, and refreshed my trust in

Story 36: Welcome to the Cuckoo's Nest

the Holy Father's direction and purpose for my life. I immediately put pen to ink to write a letter:

Dearest lovely Mindy,

I long to see your sweet face shining in the sun. You have brought warm and needed feelings into my weary heart. May our Beloved Holy One continue to watch over you and protect you at all times. His peace is stronger and purer than a thousand mountain streams. My love for you continues to blossom into a fragrant bouquet. There are so many things that I wish to share with you in word and deed, but the written word holds me fenced in with patterns of ink.

Love, Marty

My counselor, who I answered to as my direct authority, was named Dr. J.R. Lord. He got the idea that Christianity was my crutch, and decided it was his responsibility to remove this false crutch from my life. He thought I could then have a balanced, healthy life, for what he called "the real world." He was a real piece of work.

He literally got in my face one day, eyeball-to-eyeball, and yelled, "I am your Lord and you will do what I command you to do!" I was greatly distressed by his threats and obsession with control. His constant pressure on my daily life didn't let up. He seemed to go out of his way to make my life miserable. As they say, he was mean to the bone.

He took a strange pleasure in holding a symbolic sledgehammer over my head, and continually reminded me that if I screwed up, he would send me back to prison. I came to believe that he was a little on the sadistic side of therapy.

As a matter of fact, I believe many of the programs at the medical center were somewhat sadistic by design. They professionally called it *behavior modification.*

Ken Kesey, a well-known hippie from the early sixties, wrote the novel *One Flew over the Cuckoo's Nest* in 1962. Kesey based the book on his experiences at a federally financed experimental program he volunteered for as a student at Stanford University, to earn a few extra dollars.

Break on Through to the Other Side

They gave him large quantities of LSD and many other experimental drugs to see how he would react, especially during interrogations. Lobotomy, the repressive tool of absolute control in Kesey's book, is no longer used openly in America. I have heard the practice still takes place legally in many other countries.

The Oakdale medical center doctors did not use lobotomy, but they still had some very forceful and powerful tools in their arsenal for behavior modification. Shock treatment, known professionally as ECT, or electroconvulsive therapy, could fry a few million brain cells in just one session. It was used to literally trigger a seizure in the patient, or victim, depending on how you look at things. The first time I viewed the procedure, I almost threw up.

Each patient had what was called an order sheet, written up for the patient's therapy while at Oakdale. Bob Smith was an inmate who had been sent over from Anamosa prison for evaluation. His order sheet specified that he was forbidden to smoke. One day, he lit up a cigarette after lunch. Yep, that was it—he lit up a cigarette. He had violated one of the rules of his order sheet.

The alarm rang, and a nurse called for the assistance of aides who were on the floor. The aides came within a minute or two and sequestered him. According to his order sheet, he was to be delivered to the shock treatment room immediately. As they dragged him away, he yelled and screamed and begged them not to do this again to him. He cried as they strapped him onto the operating table.

They put a rubber block in his mouth, between his teeth, so that when the electricity surged through his head, triggering a seizure, he wouldn't break off his teeth with involuntary convulsing. The doctor put what looked like petroleum jelly on each side of his forehead, in the temple area, then placed electrodes there. In a loud voice, he said, "Everyone stand back, I'm going to flip the switch."

Story 37:
Apomorphine, Anyone?

I have observed through my experiences a paradox of sorts:
Not everything counts that can be counted,
and everything counted does not necessarily count;
it all depends on who is keeping the score.
—Uncle Bear

I could see Bob's eyes just before the doctor flipped the power switch. He was terrified. I had never seen such fear in a person's eyes. My instinct was to grab the doctor and throw him aside, but I knew if I did, I would be doing hard time for the next several years.

I just stood there, paralyzed, not knowing what I could do for this poor soul. The doctor flipped the switch. Bob's eyes looked like they were going to explode out of his head. His back arched, and he rose a foot or more at the waist, with only his head and feet still on the table. I could hear his teeth grinding into the rubber block.

The surge of electricity seemed to last for a long time, but it was probably only a few seconds. A life can be altered forever in a few seconds. When it was over, Bob lay on the table, limp and lifeless, his eyes glazed over, just staring at the ceiling.

The doctor took the block of rubber from his mouth and sopped up the saliva that poured out, down both sides of his face. He checked with his stethoscope to see if there was a heartbeat. Bob started to take deep breaths, but continued to stare at the ceiling. The entire experience was humbling enough, but even at that, Bob had wet his pants.

It took one aide on either side of Bob to hold him up and assist him so he could slowly shuffle his feet in an attempt to walk. I tried to talk with Bob a couple of hours later. He didn't even recognize me, nor could he speak coherently. Bob remained very passive, and his personality had changed from that day onward.

I read the doctor's notes the day after Bob's treatment: "Treatment on inmate Bob Smith was completely successful; no further treatment is necessary at this time. If any other orders in the future are broken by Bob, I recommend using apomorphine treatment."

Apomorphine was one of the drugs of choice the doctors used for their so-called treatment. In some ways, it is similar to beating the hell out of a dog for pooping on the carpet. The "treatment" is designed to remind the dog at a very deep level that if he does it again, he will get the hell beat out of him.

When a human does this to a dog, it is called cruelty to animals, and you can actually get arrested for it. When a psychiatrist or a medical doctor does this to a human, it is called therapy, and the doctor might even get a paper published in a medical journal.

Very few of the nearly one million doctors in America perform these medieval torture-type medical procedures. Remember the good old days of bloodletting? More recently, the fifty thousand plus lobotomies that were performed by psychiatrists and medical doctors, but are no longer allowed in the United States.

It is extremely important to me to make it clear—very clear—the vast majority of health care practitioners are caring, dedicated, wonderful people. Some of my dearest friends are in the medical profession. However, when money, power, and control are involved, often corruption isn't far behind.

Apomorphine! Oh yes! Apomorphine is a poisonous white crystalline alkaloid derived from morphine, and used medicinally to induce vomiting. Rumor had it that the doctors had added some other

Story 37: Apomorphine, Anyone?

compound to the crystalline alkaloid to induce not only vomiting, but also other, very unpleasant attributes similar to that of heroin withdrawal. It could be listed on the order sheet of a patient who had any perceived behavior problem. The behavior disorder could range widely, from knocking chairs over, to refusing to shave, or not tucking a shirt in before breakfast.

Bill Jones, an inmate and temporary resident at the medical center, was here for an evaluation for his upcoming parole board hearing. He was on his way to the cafeteria when a nurse requested that he come into her office. I overheard him say, "If I come into your office right now, I will miss lunch."

She replied, "There are much worse things that could happen to you than just missing one meal."

He said, "I will be happy to meet with you after lunch."

She raised her voice and demanded, "You had better get into my office immediately, and I'm not joking."

He was obviously frustrated by her untimely demand. "Ma'am, it should be listed in my medical evaluation that I am a diabetic. Ma'am, I need to eat."

Bill did have a bit of an attitude problem that the medical center was trying to modify for him. He turned away from her and said, "I will see you, ma'am, after lunch."

Her face turned red with anger, and she yelled into the hospital intercom microphone for aides to come to her unit ASAP, and be ready to sequester patient Bill Jones.

I was released from taking part in these aide raids, as they were called, because of my religious beliefs. Some of the other aides actually enjoyed the process of sequestering a poor soul. I think it gave them a feeling of power, or for some individuals, it was because they were just plain mean.

After the nurse called for aides, four came running to assist Nurse Ratched. That really wasn't her name, but many of the aides liked calling her by that name. Nurse Ratched was the fictitious demented nurse in *One Flew over the Cuckoo's Nest*.

The four aides held Bill down on the hallway floor while the nurse administered a hypodermic needle shot of apomorphine into Bill's left arm. Immediately—and I mean immediately—Bill started to throw up, and his body seized up on him as if someone had kicked him in the stomach. He writhed in pain on the hallway floor.

Nurse Ratched calmly said to the aides, "Take Bill back to his unit, and secure him to his bed. Make sure his head is turned to one side so that he doesn't choke to death on his own vomit."

Bill was sent back to Anamosa prison shortly after this episode. In the notes that Nurse Ratched had written on his order sheet it said, "Bill Jones has shown antisocial behavior and a violent attitude on a number of occasions. Has not responded to treatment, and remains insolent to authority. Our recommendation for his upcoming parole board meeting is as follows: Parole at this time is highly unadvised by our medical staff. We would like to see him again in one year for further treatment and evaluation."

Story 38:
Miracles Do Happen

*Why is it that a so-called realist sees the difficulty
in every opportunity, and the opto-mystic dreamer always seems
to see an opportunity when confronted with a difficulty?*
—Uncle Bear

I soon learned that most people in the medical center didn't fare well with the treatment they received, or the evaluations they were given. It didn't help knowing that I was the first inmate from Anamosa prison who had received a scholarship of sorts to be an aide here.

All the other aides were inmates who had once been patients at Oakdale. They had worked their way up through the system to become aides. The aides in general resented me, because I had never been a patient there, like they had.

A few of the aides continually complained about one thing or another that I had done or not done. They were beginning to set me up for various infractions of the code of conduct. It appeared to be only a matter of time before they would get me written up on false accusations.

A number of times, an aide would try to provoke me to physical violence. The old center linebacker in me was still alive, and only wanted the opportunity to cut loose and hammer my would-be offensive opponent. But I knew it would only result in my undoing and demise.

The days of wildly running head on toward a charging black bear were long gone. I missed the feeling of wild abandonment and being completely committed to the moment, without any fear or regard for the consequences. Then it occurred to me that if the black bear had not turned aside and run away, I could have very well been disfigured for life, or worse. Once again, I took a moment to thank the Eternal One for preserving my life through all the craziness of my younger days. Gratefulness is always a wonderful equalizer.

It didn't seem to matter whether the danger alert came from a physical, mental, or emotional attack. My response was to be the same: do nothing in retaliation. It was a painful learning process for me to just let it go and not react. I didn't enjoy this self-denial dying process. In my younger days I would run to a fight not retreat from it.

I had to continually practice the presence of the Presence. Being completely in the moment was the only way I could maintain an awareness of the Holy One. It was the only way I could maintain my composure.

Another way I maintained my equilibrium was through the hope of a very special joy set before me. I desperately needed a joy set before me. The hope and joy set before me was one day being with Mindy.

I contemplated and meditated upon a text found in the New Testament, "Looking unto Jesus the author and finisher of our faith; who for the joy that was set before him endured the cross, despising the shame, and sat down at the right hand of the throne of God."

After much prayer and contemplation, I came to believe that everyone needed a hope and a joy set before them. A scripture came to mind, I pondered at length the wisdom of Proverbs from the Old Testament, "Hope deferred makes the heart sick: but when the desire comes, it is a tree of life." Trusting the Eternal One regarding my possible future with Mindy and writing to her brought a wonderful calmness and peace to my heart and soul.

Sweetest Mindy,

The sound I long to hear more than anything else in the world is "Marty, I'm back again, and in your arms where I belong." *I miss hearing your lovely voice more every day.*

Story 38: Miracles Do Happen

There has been a rumor in the air around here that the parole board might be meeting with me in the not too distant future. When I'm released to California on parole, it would be so incredibly wonderful if you could come to see me. I would be on the first plane to Oregon, but then I would be back in jail for breaking my parole.

I need for you to help explain to me why I keep hearing church bells ringing, and a wedding song is continually rolling around in my head. My greatest hope is that you are hearing the same beautiful music.

Your lonely man,
Marty

I felt that I could go through anything if I could just see her again. The letters I received from her were worth their weight in gold. Mindy's letters were now arriving on a deeply appreciated regular basis.

Regardless of the spiritual warfare going on around me, and the gag order placed on me, I still had a burning desire to share the good news with someone, anyone. One day while walking down a hallway at the medical center, I saw Walter standing in his usual spot, smoking a cigarette. From day one at the hospital, I had been warned about Walter. He had been in the center for several years.

Walter would stand in the same place every day, smoking a cigarette. He never put out a cigarette when he was finished smoking it. He would let it burn itself out by holding it between his fingers, and eventually it would burn into his fingers until there was nothing left to burn.

His fingers were deranged and colored a dark blackish-brown from the years of nicotine and the constant burning. They resembled stubs more than actual fingers. His remaining teeth were a murky greenish-russet shade, and were all jagged from the various times when he would break them off by biting into a steel object, or by hitting himself in the mouth with a blunt object. Walter was in a continual state of living hell.

Walter had attacked many aides, nurses, and doctors over the years. I was told that if I should try to take away one of those cigarettes as it burned into his flesh, he would turn on me like a wild animal. His nickname among the aides was Walter the Wolfman, because of the way he would bite them in the face or on the arm, or sink his jagged teeth into their leg. On more than one occasion, he would lock onto a bite until apomorphine was injected into his body.

He was incarcerated for murdering his wife, and was facing a life sentence. His wife had become pregnant by another man during a brief encounter. She lied to Walter about the pregnancy. Walter thought the baby was his. But on a very unfortunate day, the other man returned to see Walter's wife. Walter caught them together, and she admitted that the baby was the other man's. Walter completely snapped.

He went to the kitchen and grabbed the biggest knife he could find. The man fled for his life, but Walter stabbed his wife to death, and the unborn baby died of stab wounds, as well. However, during the murder, Walter had a severe split from reality, and shortly thereafter he was deemed insane.

Day in and day out, everyone stayed clear of Walter at the medical center. But on one particular day, my eyes were opened to see him from a higher perspective. The Eternal One loved Walter, and had forgiven his sin in the same way that Christ had forgiven everyone. I knew in my knower that I was going to be used by the Beloved to help Walter.

Day after day, when I made my rounds, I would find Walter in his usual place. He would always sit on the same bench, when he wasn't smoking. No one ever dared sit with him, for fear of what he might do. Love beckoned me to sit with him. So, I did, day after day.

Usually, I would just pray for him very quietly, or softly speak in my spirit language. After doing this for a couple of weeks, I began to see and experience some unusual changes in Walter. The first changes were in some strange manifestations, through growling at me, gritting his teeth and farting. The Holy Spirit made it clear to me that these actions were from demons inside Walter.

I knew what I was doing was very risky in regard to my own prison sentence, but I felt compelled by the love of God to set Walter free from the demons that possessed him. I now had a purpose beyond just staying

Story 38: Miracles Do Happen

out of trouble at the medical center. The fear of losing my self-control had left me. I knew I was here for a reason, and Walter was that reason.

Some of the doctors and nurses noticed I was spending time with Walter. I asked them if it would be all right if I did a little experiment by reading aloud the Psalms, and maybe some other uplifting poems, or even jokes. To my surprise, they agreed with my attempts to reach out to him.

I never did get around to reading him any poems or jokes. However, within one month of reading Walter the Psalms and from the Gospel of John, there was an obvious improvement in his behavior. He would now show the slightest smirk of a smile when he saw me coming. No one could remember ever seeing Walter smile at anyone or for any reason.

Every once in a while, a demon would manifest itself. I would just quietly tell it to be silent in Jesus's name, and then I would cast it out. The demons usually came out in coughing spells and spitting. Other times, they would come out through belching or farting—the most disgusting smells imaginable. Of course, I never mentioned to anyone that I did a little casting out of demons and praying that Walter could be healed of all sorts of tormenting things.

In the second month, Walter's improvement caught the attention of the head doctor. He recommended that Walter be released to a minimum-security care facility. He was, in fact, released to that facility a month later. A few weeks had gone by since Walter had left us, and I was told that Walter was spending many hours a day outside, working in the flower garden. He had quit smoking, and he read the Psalms regularly.

Story 39:
Open the Doors

It is of great importance to realize that special times, places, and moments in life come and go swiftly, but your memories will remain. Therefore, become a master memory maker, and learn to let go of the rest.
—Uncle Bear

My time at the medical center in Oakdale was the longest and most difficult six months of my life. However, the day of my scheduled parole board meeting finally came. I had to sit in a waiting area just outside the room where the board was meeting.

Nine of us were scheduled to meet with the parole board that day. I prayed and asked the One to make a way for me to be the first to meet with them. Then a strange thought occurred to me. These observable words entered my thoughts: "Would you rather be first, or would you rather be last?"

My answer was immediate: *Yes, I want to be first.* I was a bit nervous, and I wanted to get this thing over with.

A scripture popped into my head, "The first shall be last, and the last shall be first."

I reacted unpleasantly, with these thoughts, *Father this isn't fair. I don't even know what that scripture is supposed to mean on a good day. How in the world am I supposed to interpret it today?*

Story 39: Open the Doors

My question addressed to the Eternal One was answered by yet another question. "Do you want to be first, or do you want to pray for each of these men as their lives are held in the balance?"

I quickly answered, *I still want to be first, but I get it. I will be last, because I am going to sit here and pray for each of these men, one by one.*

The first inmate was called in. I prayed for him while he met with the board. He came out of the meeting back to where the rest of us were anxiously watching to see the expression on his face. His face was red, and he was noticeably angry. He didn't say a word. He just shook his head in disbelief as he passed by us.

The second person went in, and came out with basically the same result. Except he did say, "Screw them. What the hell do they know?"

The third inmate went in, and came out just mumbling to himself incoherently.

Heavenly Father, my praying for these dear souls doesn't seem to be doing much good. What am I supposed to do for them?

"Keep on keeping on," popped into my thoughts.

Keep on keeping on! What is that supposed to mean?

"It isn't how you start a race; it's how you finish the race that matters."

OK, I'm cool with that, and what race am I running?

"Keep on keeping on." And that was that, our conversation was concluded for the time being.

The fourth man went in, came out smiling, and said, "I didn't want to get paroled anyway. I have no place to go where I can get three free meals a day, a roof over my head, a color TV, free medical, weights for working out, and friends to play cards with."

I actually wasn't surprised by his response. I had come to understand that not just a few inmates would rather stay in the care of the state than face the hard, cold world outside these walls.

The fifth inmate went in, and came out crying uncontrollably. He simply said, "I can be with my wife and kids again! I will be with them soon. I will be with them." We quietly congratulated him, and I started to weep with him. I stood up and gave him a big bear hug. Then it occurred to me that I didn't even know this guy. But it didn't matter—we were united by a fundamental love for family and home. We were being in the moment, the eternal moment.

The sixth, seventh, and eighth inmates did not receive their paroles that day. Then it occurred to me that the Good Shepherd would leave his flock to seek out and find the one lost sheep.

It was now my turn. The parole board was partially as I had expected. They did a lot of good cop, bad cop role playing.

However, the chairman of the parole board was completely over the top. He literally yelled at me in a very angry voice, "Do you realize that no one in the history of Iowa's penal system has ever been released on parole in nine months on a ten-year sentence?"

"*Yes, sir, I am aware, and I am extremely grateful to you and God for this undeserved consideration.*"

For some weird reason, that seemed to make him really upset. "What the hell does God have to do with this meeting?"

"*Well, sir, I don't believe I would be standing here today if it was not for Christ Jesus changing my life.*"

"Are you saying, young man, that your time of incarceration did not change you?"

I took a deep breath and answered, "*Yes, sir, that is what I am saying.*"

"Explain yourself, inmate Berry, before I overrule the board's decision to parole you." I think he was trying one last time to see if I would react in an angry or rebellious manner. I was very aware of the calming presence of the Presence.

I could vaguely recall a scripture that I thought Jesus had spoken. Yes! It was in the Gospel according to Matthew, where Jesus was referring to what will happen when authorities bring you up before them, and demand of you an answer for what you believe.

Jesus said something like, "Don't worry about what you will say, because the Spirit of your Heavenly Father will speak for you." I took

Story 39: Open the Doors

another deep breath and began to speak, trusting the Holy One would give me the words.

"*In my view, sir, there are two incredibly important days in everyone's life. The day you were born, and the day you ask, why was I born? However, to this day, I am amazed and dumbfounded at how many people never seem to get around to the why am I here question. They seem to live from day to day as if their daily routine will continue forever.*"

"*The why of breaking through to the other side is, in my opinion, not a matter of if, but when it happens. Many a young person has believed, hidden in their heart of hearts, that they have a spiritual origin. However, as the years go by, it seems that many people undergo some sort of spiritual amnesia.*"

"*I have no idea why so many people live their lives as if they will never die, but that they'll go on living in their current bodies forever. I have wondered countless times what is at the core of that denial. The real paradox is that everyone who is sane knows they will one day experience physical death, yet few prepare for the inevitable. The question remains, does it matter if you are in a state of denial regarding your unavoidable, ultimate eternal breakthrough, or not?*"

I paused for a moment. I could not believe the words I was saying, but I figured what the hell, you can't change horses in the middle of a stream. I took another deep breath and continued.

"*Living in denial will not solve the problem of impending death. It is for those who have not prepared, or those who are not ready for the ultimate shock of the inevitable death of their physical bodies that I groan in my spirit for their breakthrough and transformation.*"

"*I believe we have been created to live in resurrected bodies for all eternity, with God. Jesus is who He said He was. He is the Way, the Truth, and the Life. If anyone comes to Him, they will not be turned away, but received into the family of God.*"

"OK! I think we get it, young man. You believe that you have experienced this breakthrough to the other side. And I must say you are very enthusiastic, and appear very authentic in your beliefs. However, as convincing as your words are, that is not what we are here for today. We are here today to see if our penal system has changed and rehabilitated you into a law-abiding citizen.

"I am going to ask you again a very important question that will greatly affect our decision and your future. Did the penal system of Iowa change and transform you into a law-abiding citizen? Please, pause for a moment and think this through before you answer."

"*Well, sir, I deeply appreciate you and the others on the parole board for giving me this opportunity to come before you. I respect your authority over my life regarding my future accommodations. However, I must answer you honestly, and with a clear conscience.*"

"*I believe that my Heavenly Father is responsible for my transformation, and it was in fact the Holy Spirit who changed me before I got here. My experience at Anamosa prison, and here at the Oakdale medical center, have given me the opportunity to live it out in my everyday life.*"

The expressions on their faces were not exactly favorable. After a very uncomfortable silence, the board chairman spoke once again, "I see here in the official notes of your incarceration that you had a nickname at Anamosa. Is that correct, Aide Berry?"

"*Yes, sir, that is correct.*"

"Aide Berry, what did they call you?"

"*Many of my friends and a few enemies at Anamosa liked calling me the Monk, Marty the Monk.*"

He smiled broadly and said, "Well, Marty the Monk, it is my personal opinion, off the record of course, that you should continue to follow this path you have found. I am pleased to inform you that the good you have done at Anamosa has continued to this day.

"You have complied with every request that was made of you here at Oakdale, and we are aware that you did not agree with some of those requests. But you held the course, and complied with the doctors and nurses here at the medical facility. Many of the guards at Anamosa and the staff here at Oakdale have endorsed your character."

I was caught completely off guard by his encouragement to continue on the course and stay on the path.

Story 39: Open the Doors

"However, I believe I speak for all the board members in what I am about to say. We are here today to congratulate you on your well-earned parole. It is only fair that we tell you a little secret. We were fully informed before this meeting about your sincere radical commitment to your faith and your God.

"If you had told us that the penal system of Iowa had transformed you into the person that you have become, we would have known that you were lying just to get an early parole. If you had done so, we had already agreed to cancel your impending parole for being a phony. You, Marty the Monk, are anything but a phony. I just hope you're not a closet lunatic."

He extended his hand and said, "Let me be the first to congratulate you on who you have become, and on your early parole."

I stood there thanking them for their kindness and for granting me an early parole. But actually, all I could think about was that I would be seeing Mindy once again. I didn't know how it was going to work out. I just knew I had to be with her.

It was a great relief to receive a love letter from Mindy the very next day.

My love,

Such an inseparable part of me is you, my love. My desire is for you and you for me. Though at times it seems painful, as if time had stopped. The day of our reunion seems so far away. Yet I know the day will come.

I long to embrace you again, feeling safe and secure in your arms. You are my protector. Yes, you are my love. You fill my every longing of what I desire in a man. There is none other like you. Oh how I love you.

You are thoughtful, kind, true, generous, giving, loving, and yes, handsome. I wait for the day when you will be back in my arms and I in yours.

With love, your love,
Mindy

Story 40:
The New Day Begins

*Yesterday has vanished, and tomorrow is out of reach.
Being in the moment is reality,
and living in eternity is now.*
—Uncle Bear

Mindy had flown back to Switzerland by herself at the age of seventeen to attend the same five-month training course I had attended the previous year. She spent three months in Lausanne, and two months in Morocco.

All the while, Mindy's mom, Betty Rawlins, was writing letters to me about how well Mindy was doing, and how she sincerely hoped the two of us would one day be wed. She also wrote similar letters to Mindy about how well I was doing. She continually encouraged Mindy to pray for me and to wait for me.

As for the honorable Dr. Duane Rawlins, he must have been put in some kind of a *will freeze* by God. He hoped I was just a passing summer puppy love, and that I would disappear into the sunset—any sunset, as long as it was elsewhere.

August 24th was the last time I walked through the bulletproof glass doors of the maximum-security Iowa Medical and Classification Center. Though initially facing a thirty-year sentence, then having it dropped to a

Story 40: The New Day Begins

ten-year sentence, after just nine months of incarceration, I was now walking out the doors a free man.

A deputy sheriff drove me to the Iowa City municipal airport. The authorities in Iowa were happy to send me off to California with a one-way ticket. They sincerely hoped I would not return to the fine state of Iowa for a long time.

Hours earlier on the same day, August 24th, Mindy had boarded her flight from Tangiers, Morocco, to Portland, Oregon. We had not communicated with each other regarding the dates of our flights. However, the I Am had a plan for us, and we were falling into it with open arms.

I had been paroled to California because I had a construction job waiting for me. I could not leave California for any reason, as it would be a violation of my parole. So dear Betty Rawlins drove with Mindy, in her orange VW bug, one thousand miles south from Salem, Oregon, to Anaheim, California, so that Mindy could see me.

A few months later, I was granted the privilege of transferring my parole to Oregon. Mindy's family invited me to stay in their home. It was a fine home, built on a gradual slope, with a creek running behind it. The main floor of the house was at ground level. I shared the downstairs of the house with Mindy's brother, Matthew. He had his own private bedroom. I slept on the foldout couch.

It was a nice, big, open room with a fireplace. I loved building a fire there. Many a night, Mindy and I were comforted by the warmth and coziness of the flames from that fireplace. Sometimes it seemed as if the flames danced for us. Love will do amazing and wonderful things to your perception of reality.

However, an unfortunate pre-wedding disaster was about to take place. I had been through so many nerve-racking experiences and stressful situations that I had some emotional issues. I had developed a serious case of the fight or flight syndrome.

I was having a difficult time transitioning back to normal life. I was confused by my gloomy, downhearted condition. Everything was going wonderfully well, and I was about to marry the princess of my dreams. My downcast state of mind didn't make any sense at all to me.

Days before our wedding

During those emotional days, I took long—very long—walks, and talked it out with my beloved Heavenly Father. I was beginning to have serious doubts about marrying Mindy. I thought it would be extremely unfair for her to marry and then be stuck with a despondent mate.

I could see the concern on Dr. Rawlins's face. After all, Mindy was the only daughter of a well-to-do family. She could have her pick of the litter, and I was beginning to think of myself as somewhat of a mutt. She deserved a purebred young man, with a college education and a promising career. I had landed a minimum-wage job at the state facility for the mentally handicapped. At the time I thought, *Well, at least I fit in here.*

Story 40: The New Day Begins

On one of my really long walks, I was convinced that the marriage should not take place, for Mindy's sake. I tried to think of a way to tell Mindy that I was not the best for her—and that she deserved much better than me. It was now late and the sun had set. It began to drizzle, and a cold wind started to blow. The Rawlins home was on the outskirts of the city.

I had walked a few miles down a lonely country road. I had not seen another person or a car for over an hour. In the distance, I could see the headlights of a car coming toward me. As it approached, it slowed down, and then stopped next to me. The car's windows were rolled down, which I thought was odd in that it was raining and getting cold. The male driver asked me if I wanted a ride—even though he was driving in the opposite direction from where I was headed.

Out of courtesy, I approached the driver's window. As I got closer, it became obvious that he didn't have a shirt on. I could now see the car had two other occupants: two girls, one in the front seat and one in the back seat. All three of them appeared to be completely naked.

Out of shock and surprise, I asked, *"Uh, aren't you cold?"*

They laughed spontaneously and assured me they were feeling good. The girl in the back seat invited me to join her. She was fairly attractive and well appointed physically. I would not be honest, if I said I was not enticed by the lure of her to jump into the back seat and go for a wild ride.

I took a deep breath, stood up straight, squared my shoulders, and with a stammer spoke these words: *"No, no, no thanks! I'll be just fine. I'm walking home."* Having a keen perception for the obvious, I knew in my spirit this freewheeling ride with naked people was an obvious trap. I started walking as fast as I could in the opposite direction from where they were headed.

In that instant, anger rose up within me. It really ticked me off that the evil one was once again trying to destroy my life. At that very moment, a sudden bolt of energy and strength surged through my being.

Break on Through to the Other Side

My anger, which had usually gotten me into some kind of trouble or led to a broken relationship, morphed into determination.

As I headed in the right direction back to Mindy's house, I felt the presence of the Presence heavily upon me. I could actually feel courage and valor flowing into me. I was sure as hell not going to let the devil sabotage my wedding and my life. I got so pumped up with resolve that I ran the rest of the way back to Mindy.

As I stood in front of Mindy's house catching my breath, I pondered what had transpired in my life in recent years, months and days. After contemplating a large number of adventures and disasters, I prayed: *"Thank you Holy One for not only saving my life, but also for giving me a life worth living. A life with purpose, peace and a favorable future. I will be forever grateful. Your love has changed and transformed me. I will always love you."*

I was aware that he, the prince of darkness, would continue to try to ruin my life. I would most likely do some careless, unwise things in the future, but I had set my course, and knew my ultimate destination. I would do my best to continually follow the path of the Prince of Peace.

Mindy and I were married in the spring. Mindy was eighteen—young and beautiful—I was an old twenty-four.

Story 40: The New Day Begins

Young lovers get married

I was still on parole when we got married, and would remain on parole for another six months. Within a few weeks after my parole ended, we hit the road of adventure and new experiences. Our travels over the years have led us to more than fifty nations. Last year, Mindy and I learned, taught, and explored in the countries of Switzerland, France, Spain, Italy, Malta, Egypt, Israel, Turkey, and Greece.

I finished writing this book on August 24th, exactly forty years to the day I was released from the Iowa prison system. Mindy and I will be celebrating our fortieth anniversary this spring. We are returning to Switzerland to celebrate our love, marriage and life together.

Epilogue

My next book will spotlight our personal journeys and experiences around the world. Our stories will be filled with supernatural mysteries, romantic ventures, mystical paradoxes, dangerous undertakings, heartbreaking tragedies, wickedness, and immense betrayal. They will be honest, delightful, painful and true.

Marty and Mindy exploring in Egypt

Special Acknowledgments

An enormous gratitude fills my heart for my parents, Francis & Dottie Berry, who never gave up on me. My mom is a woman of strength and courage; she had to be to raise me. To this day, in her nineties, she continues to energize me with her constant love and wit.

Dear Betty Rawlins: Her faith in God and her faith in me is still a mystery beyond my ability to understand or comprehend to this day. Betty's prayers and constant encouragement through letters to me when I was behind bars gave me the courage, and quite frankly the audacity, to believe that Mindy could love me and would wait for me. I had no idea at the time, nor did Betty, whether I would be released from prison in a few months or a few years. Dear Betty fell ill, and after a long battle with cancer, passed into eternity in 1985.

Mindy's dad, Dr. Duane Rawlins, continues to love and encourage us to this present day. My heart will remain forever grateful to my father-in-grace. After Betty's passing, LeeAnn Smucker, also a widower, came into dad's life and became his wife. They are a constant inspiration to us.

Recognition and Thanks:

I want to say a genuine thank you to our dear friends who opened their homes and hearts during the writing of this book. I am truly thankful for you.

Becky Leau; Anthony Zarb-Dimech; Bob & Loretta O'Neill; John & Alexis Russell; Tom Bloomer; Ken & Diane Kurtenbach and Martin & Barbara Haueter - Hotel Edelweiss, Wengen, Switzerland.

The favorable outcome of this book could not have been accomplished without the cooperative effort and help of many people. The input, encouragement, editing skills and reviews have contributed greatly to the progress of this book.

If you would like to encourage others to read my story, it is available at Amazon.com.

In loving memory of Betty Rawlins 1929–1985

Made in the USA
San Bernardino, CA
25 June 2016